THE MEMEING
OF LIFE

THE MEMEING OF LIFE

A JOURNEY THROUGH THE DELIRIOUS WORLD OF MEMES

**TEXT BY
ANGUS HARRISON**

**DESIGN AND CONCEPT
KIND STUDIO**

LAURENCE KING PUBLISHING

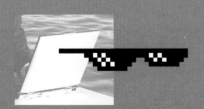

Welcome reader. Please, make yourself comfortable: pull your chair closer to the fire, put your feet up on the dog, settle your cheeks into the toilet seat. This is *The Memeing of Life*, an exhaustive, exhausting guide to the world of internet memes. Perhaps you have no idea what a meme is, so have bought this little book to expand your small mind? Possibly you're the sort of friendless berk who is already an expert but has picked up the book in order to poke holes in it? Or maybe somebody didn't know what to get you for Christmas. If so, sorry we're not a coffee machine.

The word 'meme' was first coined by the atheist academic and smarmy college-bro fan favourite Richard Dawkins, in 1976. In that simpler, pre-internet era of course, he wasn't referring to cartoon frogs or grainy images of cats reading newspapers.

'THIS IS THE MEMEING OF LIFE.'

Originally the word (from the Greek *mimeme* meaning 'something initiated') referred simply to the transfer of cultural information from person to person through writing, speech or art. Dawkins was describing the way ideas are replicated and mimicked over time with minor variations: from graffiti to musical melodies.

The spreading of a meme is like genetic evolution. An idea is passed along, and as it travels, it changes and adapts with each new connection, exploding into an endless parade of new ideas and new meanings. Unsuccessful memes will disappear into history, while successful ones can live forever.

Which brings us to the nasty, bright white soup we live in now: the internet. At some point, as humankind transitioned from the fleshy real world to the glossy digital one, Dawkins's four-letter word was itself replicated and adapted to describe internet memes. And it's these s that we are going to spend the next more than helplessly drowning in.

struggle to definitively declare the first ever meme ing to pinpoint who wrote the first knock-knock jo ch end of a garlic bread is the start and which is th ven struggle to define exactly what an internet m ith that in mind, let's set out a few ground rules f ther ...

NO.1   Typically, a meme is a combination of an image with some text – but it could be a video or even a phrase.

NO.2   The point of a meme is *almost* always to be funny.

NO.3   For a meme to become a meme it has to be shared and adapted. That hilarious picture your mum loves of a monkey drinking a glass of wine isn't a meme. That's a fridge magnet.

NO.4   The meme has to become popular, at least within a certain online community. One person sitting in their room re-editing the same picture doesn't make it a meme, however 'jokes' you think it is.

NO.5   It's meme as in dream. Not pee-pee.

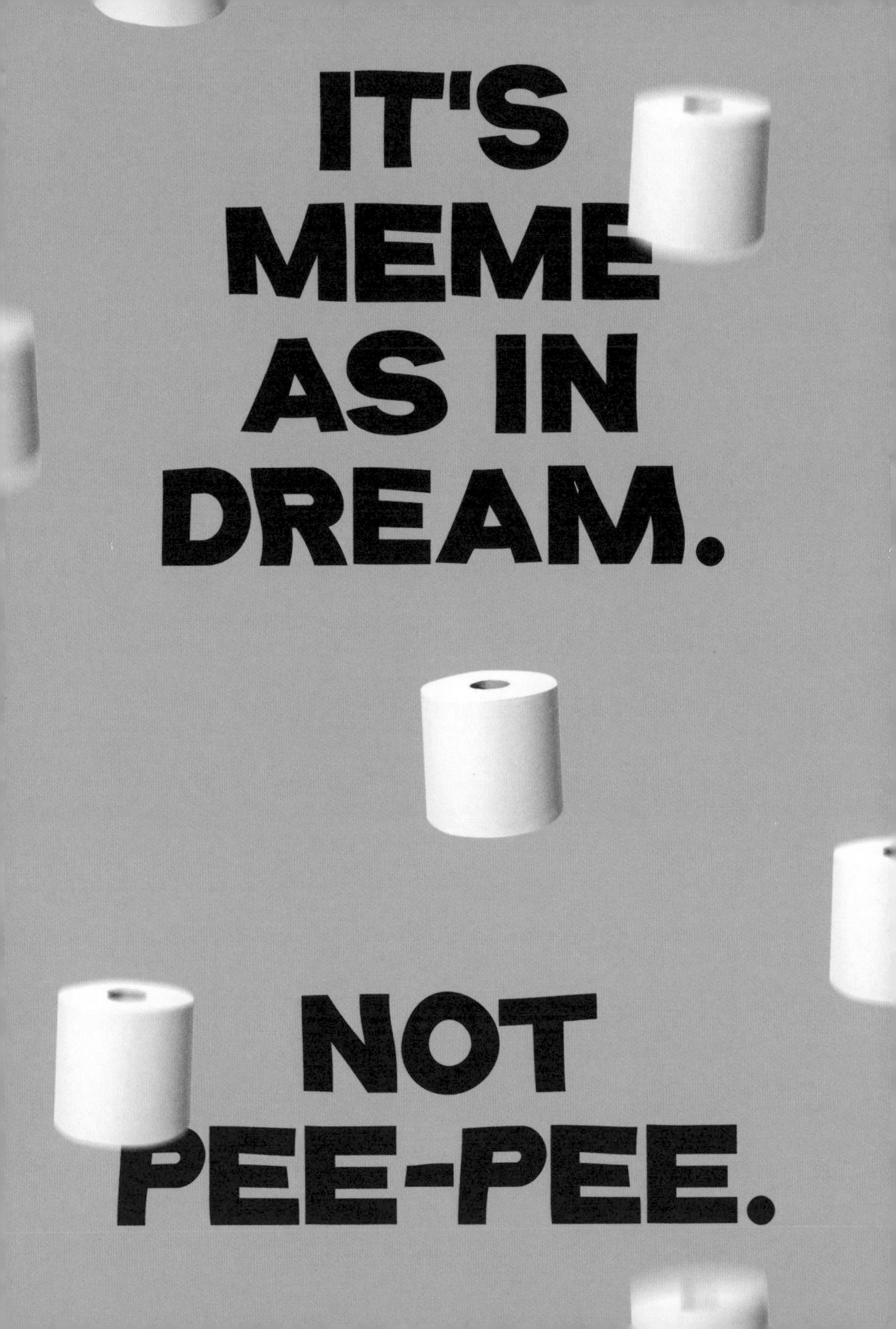
IT'S
MEME
AS IN
DREAM.
NOT
PEE-PEE.

Not that we need to tell you this. No doubt you know exactly what a meme is. The chances are you stumbled across your first in the early 2010s, somewhere between the release of *Kung Fu Panda* and the Arab Spring. The chances are it was a picture of a cat asking for a cheezburger, or maybe it was a dog on the phone. Perhaps it came up on Facebook, or you stumbled across it in the dark reaches of a forum somewhere. You probably sent it to a friend; maybe you stuck your own heading on it, all the while completely unaware you were playing a small role in a cultural revolution.

'LET'S BEGIN OUR JOURNEY DEEP INTO THE HEART OF DANKNESS, IN PURSUIT OF THE MEMEING OF LIFE.'

We now live in an era in which the internet meme rules. It has taken over – infected, seeped and dribbled into every corner of our lives. Memes about food, politics, drugs, sex, penguins and monster trucks. We are drowning in memes: endless, pointless, glorious memes. So strap yourself in – well, do whatever the book equivalent of strapping yourself in is, unless you're driving, in which case, stop reading immediately, then strap yourself into your vehicle and concentrate fully on the road – and let's begin our journey deep into the heart of dankness, in pursuit of the Memeing of Life.

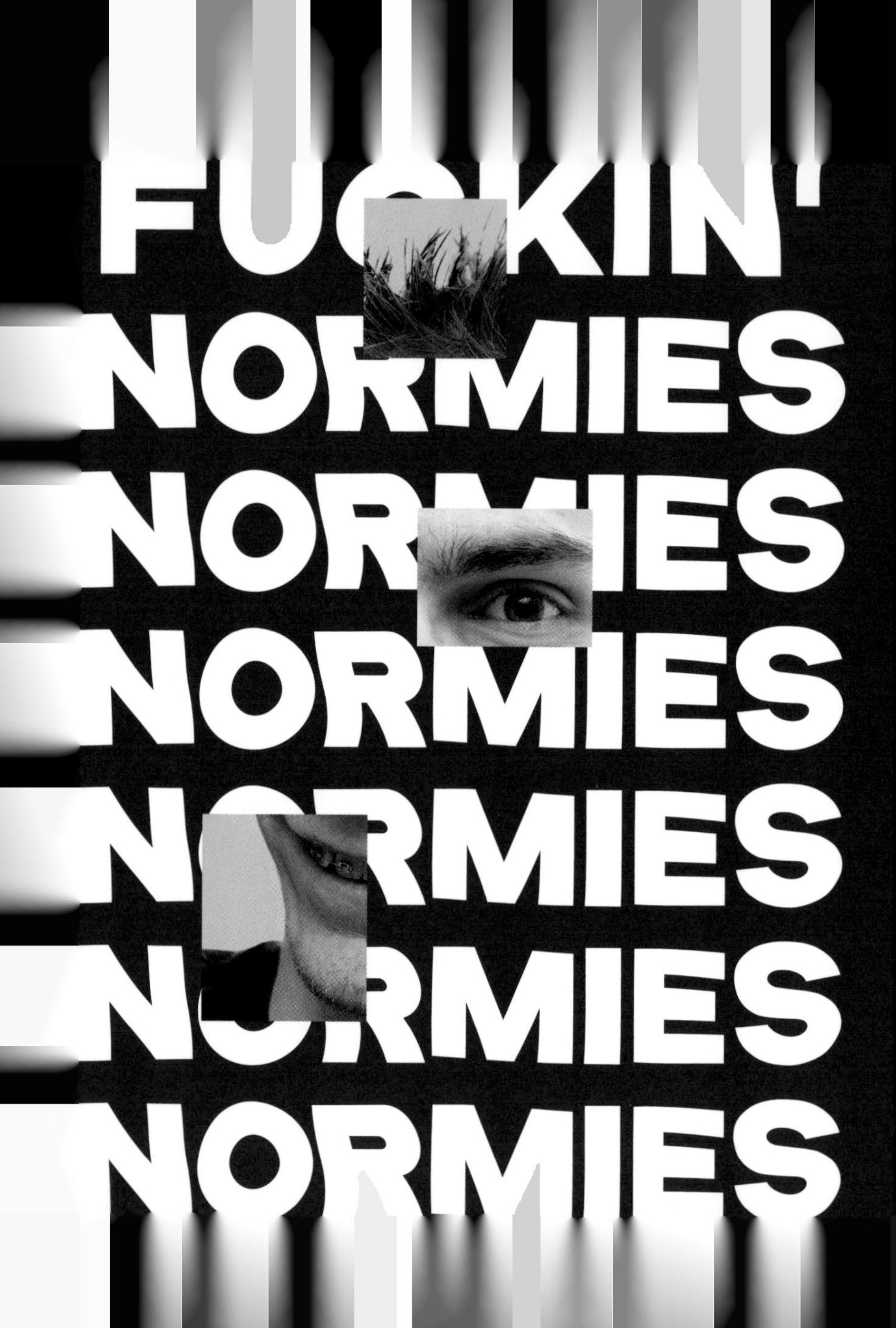
FUCKIN'
NORMIES
NORMIES
NORMIES
NORMIES
NORMIES
NORMIES

A BEGINNER'S GUIDE TO BASIC MEMES

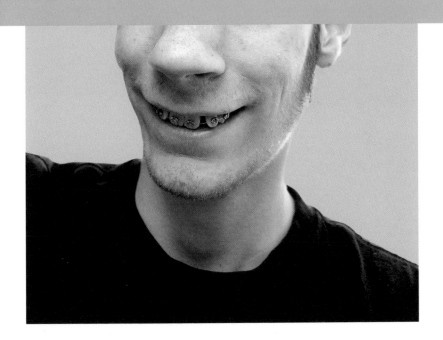

FIG. 1   DAILY MEME BUSINESS ADS

'm sorry to break it to you, but you are a normie. You probably don't even know what a normie is and here I am telling you you are one. What gives me the right? I know. Disgusting. You are, though. Sorry.

A normie – derived from 'normal' – is anyone in the mainstream who has a very basic grasp of memes. A normie lacks the judgement and restraint to enjoy memes properly. They tend to discover a meme once they've become popular, and when they do, they overuse them until they've become boring. A normie is anyone who doesn't quite get it, anyone existing outside the subcultures that are crucial to the creation and understanding of memes. Normies, we're afraid to say, ruin memes.

You don't have to be a normie, though. There is another way; but first you'll need a history lesson. And we've got just the expert to break you in.

KENYATTA CHEESE: THE ULTIMATE MEME HISTORIAN

The year is 2007. Kenyatta Cheese works in an office researching internet trends and producing content for an online video studio, and he has begun to notice something. The crudely made images with text he'd previously only seen shared over obscure forums and internet humour sites are growing in popularity. The pictures are travelling from one website to another at much greater speeds, they are popping up on Facebook, being shared by unexpected people, and even appearing in TV commercials. Memes are going mainstream.

Sensing that things were only going to get bigger, he worked with his colleagues Jamie Wilkinson and Elspeth Rountree to found Know Your Meme, an extensive and exhaustive online encyclopedia of every meme ever made. The website relies on a team of researchers, editorial staff and an online community to document memes, where they were first spotted and who made them. The site is now huge: within three years of its birth it was reaching as many as 9.5 million people a month. And Kenyatta, consciously or not, has become one of the go-to authorities on memes. Literally: he's the guy the *New York Times* or the BBC want on the phone whenever they have to explain internet humour to their audiences.

Memes have always been in his DNA, though, even before they existed. Having grown up in the South Bronx, for Kenyatta hip-hop was an early influence on the way he understands culture, especially given how the music is built on different expressions of core ideas. 'Whether it was remixing through sampling or scratching, or reinterpreting things through different mediums like emceeing, I think that for me and a lot of people I knew, memes felt familiar,' he tells us.

In the mid to late-noughties, before people talked about memes, they were already talking about something 'going viral'. Videos like 'Star Wars Kid' – a leaked recording of a Canadian high-school student wielding a golf-ball retriever like a lightsaber – had defined the lifecycle of online popularity.

The same goes for other classics, such as 'Chocolate Rain', the lyrically bizarre R&B song by musician Tay Zonday, or 'Technoviking': a video of a muscular bearded raver pounding the streets of Berlin during a music festival. These were video clips that exploded across peer-to-peer services like Limewire or Kazaa, or through exposure on websites like Funny or Die, eBaum's World, or an early YouTube.

Memes, however, remained the currency of the internet's hidden corners: sites like online imageboard 4Chan, or the satirical wiki Encyclopedia Dramatica, as well as less often referenced gaming discussion boards, and even bodybuilding forums. 'There was this weird correlation between things that became popular on bodybuilding forums becoming an internet phenomenon a few days later,' Kenyatta remembers. 'Never got to the bottom of why that was.'

These unchecked sites played host to a community of meme-makers, providing a safe place away from the mainstream for a strain of humour to emerge quite unlike anything that had preceded the internet. Mostly these jokes took the form of 'image macros', a term used to describe images with text superimposed onto them. The source material could be anything – yearbook photos, stick men, dinosaurs, penguins – and the creators, anyone.

FIG. 2

SOME OF THE MORE OBSCURE GENRES AND SUBCULTURES.

SURREAL MEMES

SURREAL MEMES ARE ARTISTICALLY BIZARRE IN APPEARANCE AND THEIR HUMOUR DERIVES FROM THEIR ABSURD STYLE.

DEEP-FRIED MEMES

MEMES WHERE AN IMAGE IS RUN THROUGH FILTERS TO THE POINT WHERE THE IMAGE APPEARS GRAINY AND STRANGE.

MONTAGE PARODIES

MONTAGE PARODIES ARE A SERIES OF REMIX VIDEOS PARODYING THE 'VIDEO GAME MONTAGE', CHARACTERIZED BY QUICK-PACED EDITS AND LOOPED FOOTAGE, AS WELL AS HEAVY USE OF LOUD DUBSTEP.

'People would make a quick meme in Photoshop or MS Paint. You'd even get people using Microsoft Powerpoint. They'd throw some text over it and screenshot that shit. It was so simple.' Of course, nothing stays hidden forever. Memes were about taking something general, and making it specific. Which is why the people who make them get defensive about normies; because meme culture, at its heart, is small.

It's organic and person to person, as particular and specific as it is far-reaching. So when the mainstream gets a look in, people feel like something secret has been spoiled: whether it's normies spamming a good meme to death on Facebook, or an advertising agency stealing a format without crediting the minds who made it in the first place.

That's why Know Your Meme was founded. 'Having watched hip-hop go from my cousin spinning two decks in his bedroom to the highly profitable product it is now, I know what happens to subcultures. I saw Know Your Meme as a way to make sure the context of memes was in a place people could find. Credit where credit is due.'

The website does the job to this day, trawling through image histories and contributor submissions to make sure every meme is recorded and every creator in the community is credited. Which is the most important thing about memes. For all their snarkiness, weirdness and cliqueiness, they are about communities, however large or small.

'Whatever it is that you're sharing, you're putting it into your network in the hope that the people around you are going to recognize something in it. That they get what you're trying to express, and if they feel similarly or get an emotional reaction out of it – they find it funny, horrifying, it pisses them off – they are prompted to push it out to other people who will recognize that experience.'

As Kenyatta sees it, the only real way of being caught out as a proper normie is if the memes you share don't mean anything. There's no right or wrong way of doing it, as long as it gets you in the feels – from mums sharing Minion memes, to the armies of dankness.

'Whether it's people who feel threatened by the normies, or people you'd maybe see as a normie, all of a sudden they have something to belong to, to feel pride about.' Understanding memes, at its core, couldn't be easier. Which is good news for you, eh? You fuckin' normie.

o.O WHAT TEH F*CK ARE LOLCATS? O.o

The practice of laughing at pictures of cats – or rather, pretending to laugh at pictures of cats other people with a limited sense of humour have sent you – feels as old as the internet itself. In fact, it's a tradition that precedes the internet by more than a hundred years. The English photographer Harry Pointer, who died in 1889, was one of the first people to force kittens to debase themselves by dressing them up in pyjamas or squashing them into pushchairs for the entertainment of the masses. The weird old bastard.

Since the dotcom boom, cats have been gently purring alongside pretty much every major online development, acting as a kind of spirit animal to the march of internet progress. They've always been there. YouTube's co-founder Steve Chen uploaded a video of his cat to the streaming service in 2005 (the year the website was started), and by

(= 0 人 0 =)ノ

2015 CNN estimated there were 6.5 billion pictures of cats on the internet. I tried counting how many cat videos are on there now but passed out at 15,433.

Yet not all pictures of cats are born equal. Or at least not all of them are LOLcats. LOLcats, specifically, are a category of image macro memes birthed on 4Chan in the mid-2000s. They combined pictures of cats with text, allowing the pets to articulate all sorts of things. With the right caption, they were hungry, depressed, sarcastic or hung-over: it all depended on the creator's angle. LOLcats constituted one of the first real meme movements. They crystallized the form of taking a picture and reapplying new contexts over and over again, cat after cat after cat.

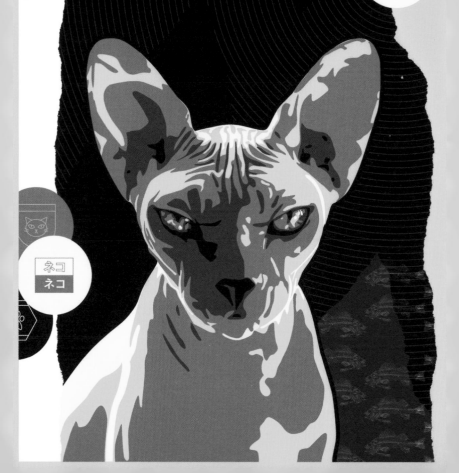

FIG.3 *LEARN TO LOLSPEAK*

BORROW THE SPELLING OF CERTAIN PARTS OF ONE WORD TO
MISSPELL ANOTHER WORD THAT SHARES CERTAIN PHONETIC SOUNDS
(OR THAT JUST RHYMES). YOU CAN ALSO MISSPELL WORDS,
REPLACING SOUNDS WITH OTHER LETTERS. LIKE 'TH' WITH 'F' OR
'Y' TO 'EH' AND ADDING 'S' TO CERTAIN WORDS.

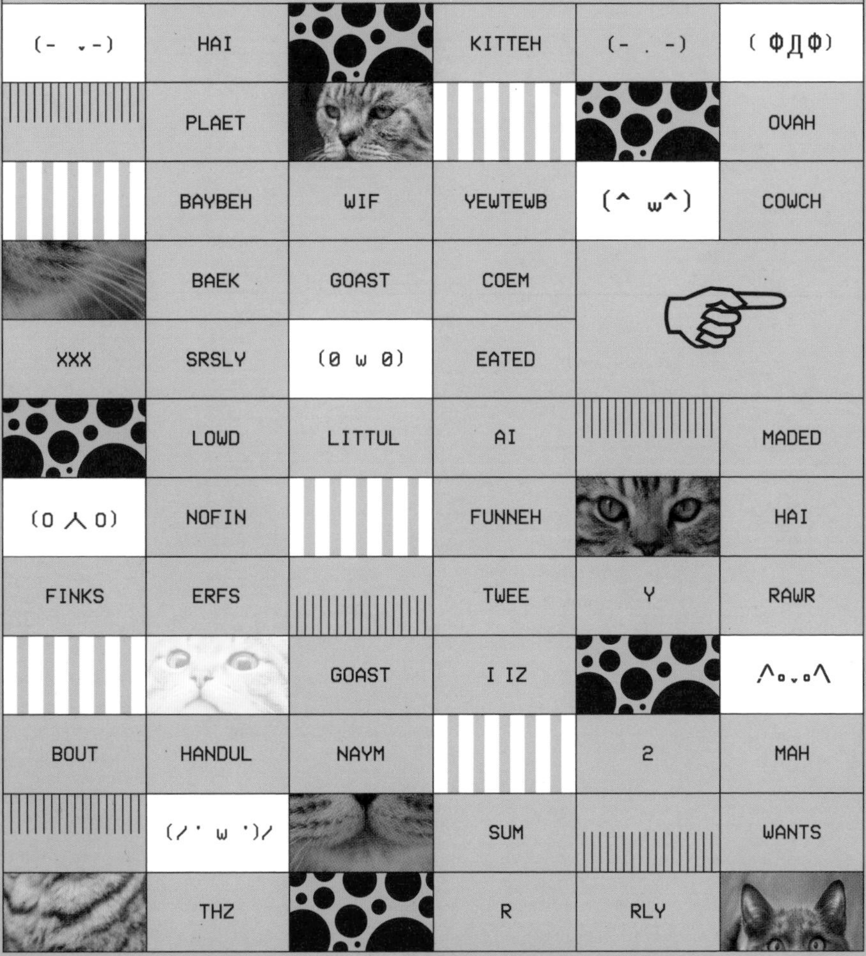

(- ˎ-)	HAI		KITTEH	(- . -)	(ФДФ)
	PLAET				OVAH
	BAYBEH	WIF	YEWTEWB	(^ ω^)	COWCH
	BAEK	GOAST	COEM		
XXX	SRSLY	(0 ω 0)	EATED		
	LOWD	LITTUL	AI		MADED
(0 人 0)	NOFIN		FUNNEH		HAI
FINKS	ERFS		TWEE	Y	RAWR
		GOAST	I IZ		∧ₒᵥₒ∧
BOUT	HANDUL	NAYM		2	MAH
	(ʅ˙ ω ˙)ʃ		SUM		WANTS
	THZ		R	RLY	

LOLcats also proved a breeding ground for a lexicon, a way of speaking on the internet that defined the early days of meme-building. 'Lolspeak' is a strain of grammatically incorrect, broken English that is particularly fucking stupid when you imagine that a cat is saying it. In fact, the language can probably best be described as an approximation of what cat owners (with too much time on their hands) think their cats might sound like, if they could talk. 'Hi' becomes *hai*, 'the' become *teh*, 'have' becomes *haz*, 'kitty' become *kitteh*, and so on. It's a language that arguably formed the basis of an entire online dialect.

The popularity of LOLcats grew, and then reached its apex with the genesis of Caturday – a tradition of posting LOLcats on 4Chan every

'TEH CATZ R GOIN NOWHERE, BUT WE'VE GOT BIGGA TINGS TO FINKS BOUT.'

Saturday, which soon spread across the internet. In its wake, cat memes have become a backbone of internet humour, almost unnervingly so. (I mean, does everyone find cats that funny? I can't be the only person who doesn't, right? I mean, they're okay, but not as funny as, say, walruses.)

'The internet doesn't actually love cats,' Kenyatta reckons. 'It's just that there's this hyperdense, super well-connected cat meme industrial complex that exists. They're so well connected and are so familiar with what they all love, that if you put the right piece of content somewhere into that network, then the likelihood of it blowing up is fairly high.'

Regardless, they are ubiquitous, and crucial to understanding the mechanics of how memes work. More than anything else, Kenyatta recognizes their staying power as totally unique. 'No matter what has happened with other image macros, those still remain the same, which I think is really interesting.' The cats are going nowhere. But we've got bigger things to think about.

CHAPTER 2

TL:DR

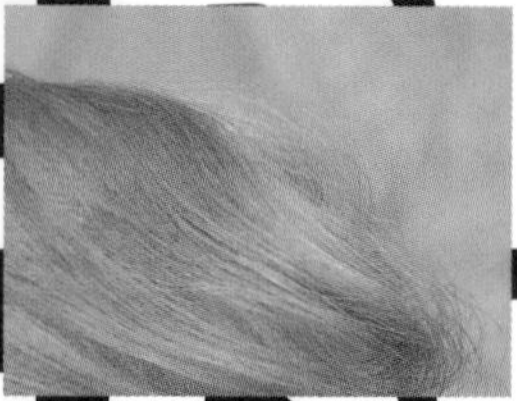

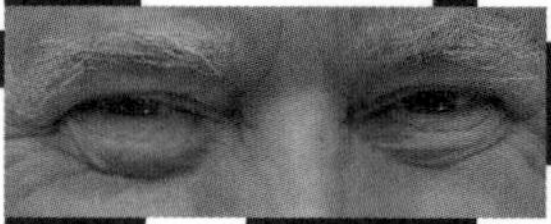

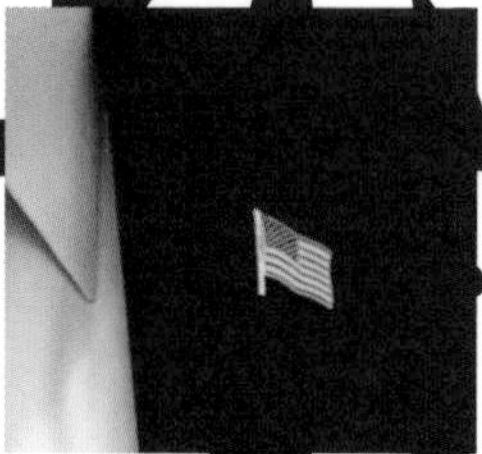

TL:DR
TL:DR
TL:DR
TL:DR
TL:DR

THE TRUTH BEHIND POLITICAL MEMES AND HOW THEY CHANGED THE WORLD FOREVER

So now you know what a meme is. (Funny pictures, people share them over the internet.) Big deal, right? I mean sure, they might be amusing, but it's not like they could ... I don't know ... influence elections or play a role in provoking seismic political events or anything. Could they? Oh dear.

Welcome to the second and most serious of chapters, idiot reader. How Memes Changed the World, or How Memes Are Taking Over the World, or How Memes Broke Democracy, or 'The Political Bit'.

'CATS. THEY CAN BE WEAPONIZED FOR GOOD, EVIL AND EVERYTHING IN BETWEEN.'

Okay, so in truth, memes can't be credited with upending the entire world order on their own, but as the global political landscape has changed rapidly and radically in the 2010s, it's important to consider the role the silly, pointless internet has played in all this. The ways in which we share and consume information have changed entirely. We no longer rely on the television or our parents to tell us what's going on in the world, why we should care, and who we should vote for. Now we get our news (real or otherwise) from each other: links, tweets, petitions, videos and, of course, memes. Which means memes are no longer only good for cats. They can be weaponized for good, evil and everything in between.

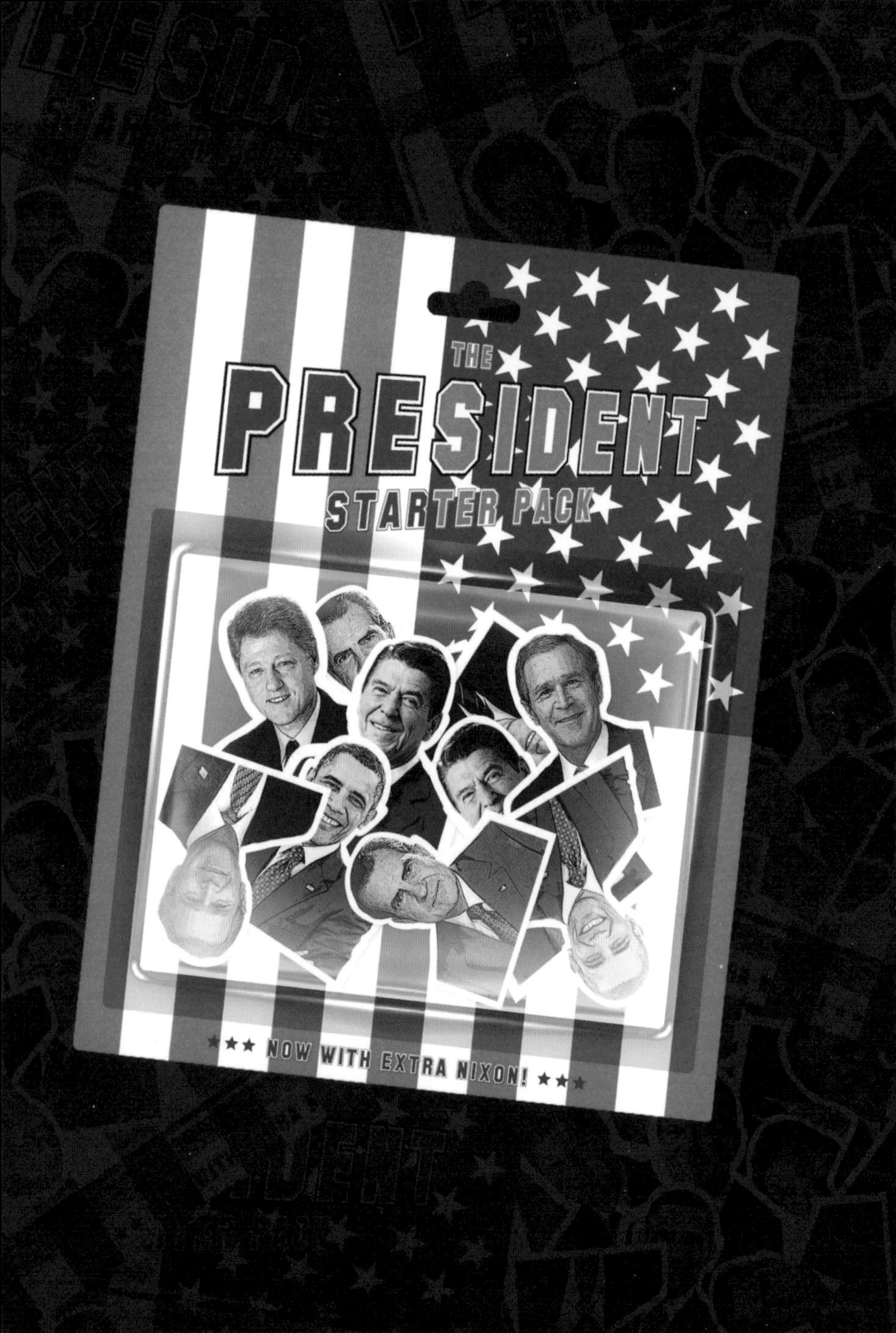
THE
PRESIDENT
STARTER PACK
NOW WITH EXTRA NIXON!

HOW HAVE MEMES CHANGED THE WORLD?

Hussein Kesvani is a journalist who writes about politics and internet culture, so we asked him some questions about both of those things, duh.

AS FAR AS YOU CAN TELL, WAS THERE A MOMENT WHEN MEMES STARTED TO GET POLITICAL?

I think memes have always been 'political', though maybe it's only now that everything is about politics. When you think about what a meme is, it's a universal mode of communication – a language that expresses a mood, or an idea that can translate across the world. When LOLcats were a thing, I don't think most people would have seen them as political, but they were one of the first memes that were adopted and heavily used by baby boomers on the internet. The fact that a meme crossed a generational divide in a way that hadn't been seen on such a big scale before is a political act, because it turned the internet into a place where communication could take place on a wider scale. And, of course, with more people sharing, more data was being shared too. If you look at what's happened in recent years with Cambridge Analytica, or Facebook openly using personal data to tweak our online experiences, it's not that much of a stretch to think that the idea at least developed from the culture created out of LOLcats.

Obviously, the most overt use of political memes began far later, and grew exponentially during the 2016 US election with Pepe the Frog memes, but it wasn't anything novel. It was more that the platforms used increased in number and, of course, in scale.

WHY DO WE TURN TO POLITICAL MEMES? WHAT CAN THEY SAY THAT OTHER THINGS CAN'T?

I think it's about group mentality, and the idea that we come online to not be alone. It's fun being part of a group or an online community, having in-jokes and building relationships based on those things that we inherently know about each other. It's comforting to see other people feel the same, and that you don't have to explain your emotions to them. They already know. And of course, that's part of wider internet culture and the nature of connectivity anyway.

ON WHICH WEBSITES HAVE POLITICAL-MEME COMMUNITIES FERMENTED?

It's different for different online communities. 4chan was obviously a big place for memes to ferment. What was interesting was that for a long time, /b/ [4Chan's 'random' message board] was considered 'the worst place on the internet' for everything from weird anime porn to racist and misogynistic opinion. It was messy, unorganized and cluttered, but it was also posited as a free-for-all. /Pol/ [the politics messageboard] has now overtaken it, and is very different in that it focuses on politics. The forum is organized just to talk about, and reinforce, right-wing political ideas rather than all the stupid and weird stuff that used to break that apart.

Other politics memes are created on other social platforms. Tumblr has always been a big one for LGBTQI+ communities. They use Tumblr because it's difficult for older generations to figure out how to use it, but also because the platform is pretty secure and offers a lot of privacy. Facebook and Twitter are used to spread memes rather than create them. (Facebook has niche meme groups but they tend to do more alterations of existing memes than actually creating new ones.)

ARE THERE PARTICULAR IDEAS OR IDEOLOGIES THAT WORK WELL IN MEME FORM?

Honestly, things surprise me all the time. Scottish independence campaigners were able to use memes ranging from anti-union jokes to Irn Bru references in ways that were comedic and non-threatening, which was the biggest risk you could take when having a nationalist party leading the campaign. Jeremy Corbyn's Labour Party in the UK has also used memes well, in order to make democratic socialism more palatable

and normal in British politics. Then look at hyper-nationalist campaigns in Italy, Brazil, India – ones that really reinforce the idea of nationality and patriotism. I think any political movement that is internationalist, and can also allow people to feel they aren't alone, will always do well, irrespective of the format.

WHAT INFLUENCE HAVE THEY HAD ON THE TONE OF DEBATE? HAVEN'T THEY JUST MADE THINGS FUNNIER?

Initially, who didn't like LOLcats, or politicians musing over the colour of The Dress? But I think that was also a time when we thought more innocently about the internet. We now have a more cynical view of the internet, at least in a political sense – part of that is because the widening of internet access encourages it. Memes that degrade politicians and, more commonly now, political activists, are always popular. I can't think of a meme that's genuinely been funny and has still allowed politics to be conducted respectfully.

WHAT'S AN EXAMPLE OF A PARTICULAR MEME SPREADING A CERTAIN MESSAGE REALLY WELL?

One person who really won on the social media front was Narendra Modi. His social media strategy was considered one of the most sophisticated in Indian politics. Some of the memes used in his campaign were hilarious and relatable, while others portrayed

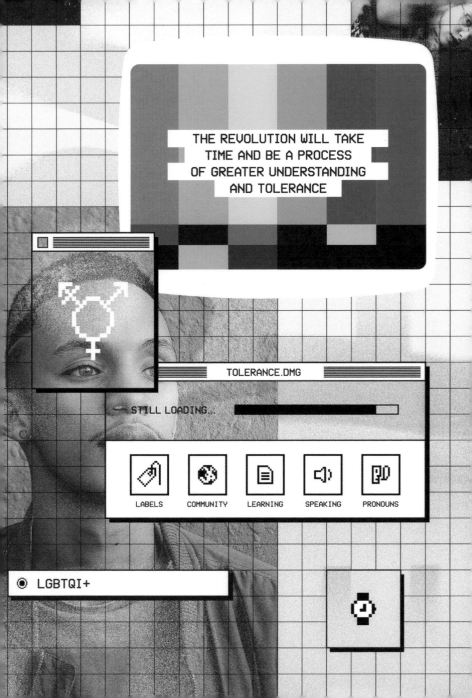

THE REVOLUTION WILL TAKE
TIME AND BE A PROCESS
OF GREATER UNDERSTANDING
AND TOLERANCE

TOLERANCE.DMG

STILL LOADING...

LABELS   COMMUNITY   LEARNING   SPEAKING   PRONOUNS

⊙ LGBTQI+

him as a strong and powerful leader, willing to take on the country's rich liberals in New Delhi, and religious groups. He also succeeded because of how fast those memes spread – not just on Facebook, but on WhatsApp, which is hugely popular in India among the older generations. And interactions on WhatsApp, because of how personalized they are, are far more likely to build trusting, familiar relationships that can end up translating to votes and activism.

HOW RELIABLE ARE MEMES FOR SPREADING INFORMATION/FACTS?

They aren't reliable. Fake news sites, as well as hyper-partisan news sites, can use memes to sell distortions of political actors and policies. The point is that a meme isn't supposed to spread facts or information; it's supposed to spread broader ideological ideas in which the facts don't matter. It's about the feeling you get from sharing and being part of a community. It's why meme-makers don't really care when people point out that they're spreading fake news. For them, news was never the point.

DO WE TAKE MEMES SERIOUSLY ENOUGH AS A POLITICAL FORCE YET?

I think we do now. I know Clinton is mocked for the Deplorable stuff, but when the (then) front runner of the presidential election talked about Pepe the Frog on live TV, and when the EU is considering how to restrict

memes in political races ... you know it's being taken seriously, even if the approach is probably misguided.

IS THIS WHAT POLITICAL DEBATE LOOKS LIKE NOW, OR WILL WE GROW OUT OF IT?

Political debate hasn't changed that much; it's just that we have a new language to express things. We've always made dumb jokes about politics, but before it was just to ourselves or friends and colleagues while watching a TV screen. It was inconsequential. Now we can say stuff on Twitter, and post memes and alterations online to reach a larger audience. I imagine that's here to stay. I can't really envision a world where we'll suddenly go back to subtle response-to-the-TV style of political engagement.

The question really is about whether platforms will take the personal safety of users seriously at such a scale, and whether there will be a point where we decide, voluntarily, to log off. IMO that's much more of a demographic question and it's one rooted in who will actually be able to *afford* to log off in the future. In the end, I reckon it'll always be the case that those with the least to lose – rich, white, urban-dweller types – will be the ones who can afford the 'digital detox'.

THANKS OBAMA: REMEMBERING THE FIRST MEME PRESIDENT

When we talk about the first-ever meme president, there's every chance somebody else will spring to mind, but resist. You'd be a damn fool to think DJT was the first politician to benefit from the spread of image macros. You see, Barry Obama, the 44th President of the United States of America, was sworn into office in 2009 – the same year Keyboard Cat burst onto the scene and Kanye dropped his seminal 'imma let you finish' line at the VMAs. Obama's was a presidency that began on the cusp of the meme explosion, and his tenure as leader of the free world was always destined to be defined by meme-friendly moments, thanks both to his armies of online supporters, and to his office's own understanding of how to play the social media game.

The first sign of how memeable Obama's time in office would be came during his campaign. In 2008, street artist and founder of skateboard clothing label OBEY, Shepard Fairey, designed a poster based on a photo of Obama, turned into a blue, red and beige stencil, with the word 'HOPE' emblazoned across the bottom. Despite not being an official campaign poster, it quickly emerged as the iconic image of his march to the White House, and in doing so became a kind of proto-political meme. The colour scheme and the artwork's blocky style made it perfect for parody, encouraging internetty dweebs to switch Barry's face for anything and everything, from Bob the Builder to Colonel Sanders to Snoop Dogg, with the word 'HOPE' changed to a more suitable caption. It was an early indicator that bored people with Photoshop were about to change the political landscape entirely. If only we knew then what we know now. Derp.

Throughout his eight years as Boss of the States, there were countless moments during speeches, foreign visits and dinners that sent the worldwide web into a tailspin. On a state visit to the UK, while meeting the Queen, Barack and Michelle Obama were both photographed pulling a 'not bad' sturgeon face, which went on to be adapted as a Rage Comics illustration. In 2012, on a trip to an Irish pub in Washington, Obama was photographed clutching a pint of Guinness and throwing a bleary-eyed thumbs-up across the bar, looking like everyone who ever made the mistake of thinking pint number six was 'doable'. In 2016, at the end of his last-ever White House Correspondents'

FIG.4   *WHICH OBAMA ARE YOU?*

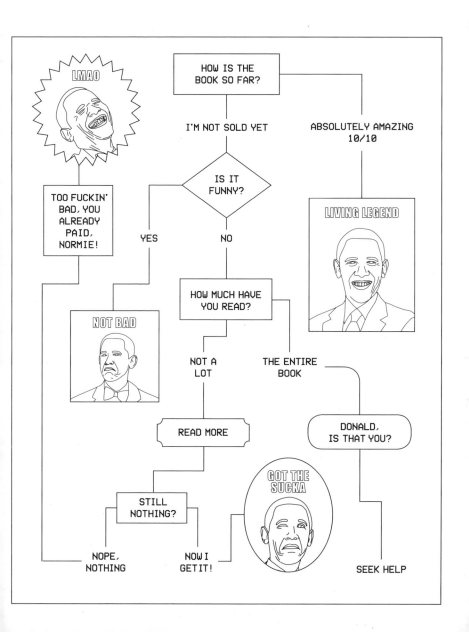

9 **FOR MEMES**

6ᶜ

Thanks Obama.

5ᶜ

U S A

4 BIDEN

AIRMAIL

1O POST

FOR HEALTHCARE
HEALTHCARE
HEALTHCARE
HEALTHCARE
HEALTHCARE

FROM

FOR THE

27. 9.94

MEMORIES

Dinner speech, Big Barry ended proceedings with the words 'Obama out', before pulling off the first-ever mic drop in presidential history. Practically everything Obama did was meme-worthy, from taking selfies to killing Osama Bin Laden. (Yes, there are Bin Laden death memes. Think that's bad? Wait until you get to chapter 4.)

Of course, none of this was accidental. Obama was an internet president and his team knew it. Within the first few years of his presidency, he had a Facebook page, a Tumblr account, had begun hosting virtual town hall meetings and taken part in a Reddit Ask Me Anything interview. At the time of writing, his Twitter account has 103 million followers to the Donald's 55 million. (Although I'm sure the Donald will see those numbers differently ... somehow.)

Inevitably, it wasn't all love and appreciation. As you may have noticed, Obama had a few detractors during his time. They found their home under the banner 'Thanks Obama', a sarcastic phrase used by haters who felt the president was robbing them of their God-given freedoms and hard-earned money. Increasing taxes? Thanks Obama. Snooping on my emails? Thanks Obama. Global financial crash? Thanks Obama. Quickly, though, the phrase was turned back on those very same Republicans who liked to blame everything on Obama, becoming an ironic response to any number of totally unrelated incidents.

Dropped my phone? Thanks Obama. Burnt my toast? Thanks Obama. Hole in my shoe that's let in water and turned the ends of my toes the same colour as my socks? Thanks Obama. In the end, Barry had the last laugh, recording a video for Buzzfeed in which he sarcastically thanked himself for a cookie that was too big to fit in a glass of milk.

Obviously, his presidency is now history, but it's been immortalized in the form of memes. During the handover period between Obama and President-elect Donald Trump, meme-makers set about turning his friendship with vice-president Joe Biden into a meme. The recurring joke usually saw Biden suggesting a prank, such as throwing a football at Trump, to which Obama would respond with a flat denial of 'Joe'. Other memes see Biden suggesting he offer Trump a knuckle sandwich, or joking that he's left a Kenyan passport in the president's desk drawer to fuck with him. This final series of memes came loaded with anxieties about Obama's successor, and stands as a fitting end to the political career of the First Meme President of the United States.

DO NOT

MY CHIL

121 PAG

GO. IT W

BE OVE

FEAR

D. ONLY

ES TO

ILL ALL

R SOON.

HOW MEMES BECAME AN OUTLET FOR DESPAIR AND ANXIETY

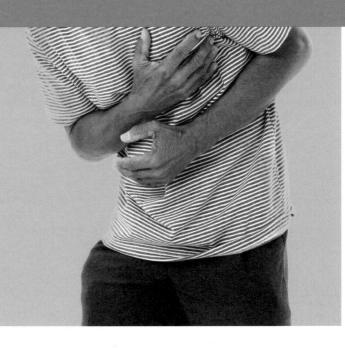

So you see: everything sucks. Honestly, it does. The world is falling apart at the seams like a cheap pair of trainers; you can't sleep because that one embarrassing thing you did eight years ago continues to roll ceaselessly around your head; you don't have as many friends as you used to, and you barely like the ones you have left. You're too old to be carefree but too young to have anything worth caring about. Your latest health kick started with the purchase of an expensive blender and ended with extra garlic mayo, cheese and a bit of chilli sauce (but not too much). Even your phone finds your life so exhausting its battery can barely stand to be alive for longer than an hour every day.

It's a grind, isn't it? A half-life lived between notifications, an online existence spent drifting through a stream of breaking news and photos of other people having more fun than you. I know. I'm sorry. Let's hug it out. Hug the book. Pop a bookmark in and hug the fucking book.

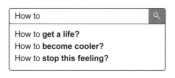

It might sound over the top, but ask any person under the age of thirty-five and they'll tell you: life isn't all roses. In fact, it's not even all dandelions. We are living through an era of extreme anxiety, both globally and personally, and to make matters worse we are living it through social media, the best and worst thing that ever happened to us, a constantly refreshing matrix of social pressure from every possible angle. We know what everyone is doing as they are doing it, yet we've never felt further apart. What, if anything, can save us from this state of chronic despair?

Memes, baby.

How to fix my life?

FIG. 5   A COLLECTION OF BINCH CITY MEMES

SO, WHO IS ACTUALLY MAKING MEMES ABOUT MENTAL HEALTH?

New York-based student Julia Hava is on Instagram as Binch City. She began the account in October 2016 as an outlet for memes she was making for her friends about mental health. She quickly found that they were striking a chord. 'I remember that people I went to school with would come up to me and tell me they felt like I was reading their mind or something.' Safe to say, the operation is now considerably bigger than her schoolfriends: at the time of writing she has more than 50,000 followers.

WHERE DOES THE HUMOUR IN ANXIETY ACTUALLY COME FROM?

'I've always been the kind of person who tries to laugh at the hard things in life as a coping skill,' Julia says. 'When I made my Instagram I was going through a really tough time mentally, and I just felt so shitty that it was almost comical. I wanted to make fun of it and be self-aware about the kinds of negative thoughts and behavioural patterns that I had.'

From images of Teletubbies lamenting their existence over bowls of Tubby Custard, to stock images recaptioned to meet the realities of contemporary dating, her account is an extension of this principle. She shares personal experiences and feelings in a way that is funny and instantly recognizable, hence her huge following, who find her memes both hilarious but also strangely comforting. 'There are a lot of universal experiences and sentiments that I wouldn't have thought would be experienced so widely,' she continues. 'Sometimes I post something and I don't know how it's going to do because maybe I'm the only one who feels this way or has this thought, but that's usually never the case.'

While the internet might be responsible for much of the mess we find ourselves in, it seems memes – these strange jokes that we pass from friend to friend, from inbox to inbox – have become an antidote: a weird cream to rub on our psychological wounds when the going gets tough. And it's not just Julia. Instagram is full of accounts that plumb the depths of personal crisis in search of spicy memes, many of which have tens of thousands of followers. Then there's the soul-searching Subreddit Me_IRL, which more than a million readers enjoy for its self-deprecating content and which has spawned an entire language of online despair.

There are memes about staying awake all night posting memes, memes about giving up on existing, memes about men who make you feel small, memes about bad skin, memes about remaining totally unloved and untouched by other human beings until the end of your days, memes about zoning out and drifting off to other planets during class, and memes about touching wet food in the sink. If something bad has happened to you, there's a meme for that, my friend.

'IF SOMETHING BAD HAS HAPPENED TO YOU, THERE'S A MEME FOR THAT, MY FRIEND.'

That's not to mention the entire meme pages devoted to specific mental health issues: anxiety, personality disorders, dissociation and depression. And wrapped around each of these pages are teens and young adults finding both humour and community in how shitty things can get for them. Memes have even been endorsed by mental health awareness organizations, such as Headspace, who described them as a positive, 'non-clinical' way of approaching problems and breaking down taboos.

The question remains, though: why memes? If every other part of the internet stresses us out, and memes are responsible for the downfall of Western democracy, how come they are so helpful when it comes to mental health? Julia reckons it's all about sharing.

'When a meme is relatable it seems as if someone was reading your own personal thoughts or observing your own life and then made a joke about it. A lot of people think their experiences are rare or unique, and I think that can make people feel isolated in their mental illness, like no one is experiencing the same kind of pain and suffering as them.'

Through pages like Julia's, people who are struggling can take comfort in knowing they're not alone, something that often leads them to seek help and guidance from other places. 'I think that joking about mental health allows people to take themselves less seriously and put their problems into perspective a little bit, but I also share a lot of

mental health resources that have helped me personally, as well as other useful information,' she tells us. 'I want to make sure people aren't just laughing at their problems but also handling them in a healthy way.'

Whether they are bringing down governments or providing comfort, sharing memes makes us feel part of something bigger. And when we feel part of something bigger, bigger things feel smaller. 'Memes have a lot of power to influence people in terms of how they see themselves and their problems,' Julia adds. 'I think they can help people learn not to internalize everything, but understand that some experiences suck universally.'

Honestly, it's not just you. Everything is terrible. Can totally relate.

When it comes to memes for the downtrodden and browbeaten, for the losers and the loners, one face, one name reigns above all others. That name is Bad Luck Brian. Well, actually, his name is Kyle. You see, in 2010 an Ohio student called Ian posted a goofy photo of his buddy Kyle Craven to Reddit. The photo of Kyle in a tartan v-neck, flashing what can only be described as a 'bracing' smile, was the epitome of teenage gawk – goofy and hapless. It was taken for his school yearbook, but in the hands of the internet it was quickly redubbed 'Bad Luck Brian', becoming a vessel for all things unfortunate.

The format of the meme is simple. Brian attempts something, and the worst possible outcome follows. Tries to fart stealthily in class? Shits. Downloads one song illegally? Prison. Has a pet rock? It runs away. Bad Luck Brian is a symbol of misadventure, disappointment and the sort of crushing fuck-my-lifery that has probably characterized so much of your life. It's an important artefact in our journey, as one of the first image macros to go truly mainstream, but also as an example of a meme that has had the staying power still to be remembered many years after its inception.

Fortunately for Kyle himself, his life isn't as terrible as his face-sake. Be-

coming one of the biggest memes in the world has actually worked out pretty well for him, turning him into something of an internet celebrity. Don't believe us? Well he's on the line now!

KYLE? ARE YOU THERE?

Hey, how's it going?

HEY BRIAN... SORRY, KYLE. SO, TELL US ABOUT YOURSELF.

Well, I live in Akron, Ohio, which is right outside Cleveland. I'm in construction for a living and I own a construction firm with my father, it's a family business. We build religious facilities, non-profits, nursing homes, car dealerships, everything. I've been doing that my whole life, and then some Bad Luck Brian stuff as well. I'm twenty-nine, I've been married for five years, I have a daughter and a son on the way.

BRIAN! CONGRATULATIONS!

Thank you!

SO WHAT'S THE STORY BEHIND THE FAMOUS PHOTO?

We took the photo to try and get it into our school yearbook. It was obviously a joke to us, which most people don't realize; I rubbed my eyes and got the stupid sweater-vest the day before. It never made it into the yearbook because my principal said absolutely not. She and I weren't on good terms anyway because I used to mess around a lot in high school and got in trouble. I was notorious for screwing around with the yearbook. My freshman year was normal but sophomore year, I have two photos back to back of myself. It was Kyle Craven underneath one photo, and then next to that it's Kyle Craven again with another photo of me. I knew the right people in yearbook department to make it happen.

SO HOW DID YOUR JOKE YEARBOOK PHOTO END UP ON REDDIT?

My best bud Ian posted it to one of the meme generators back in 2012. He left me a voicemail that night saying, 'Hey, no big deal, but I made you famous, check out this link.' I think at that point it was trending on the front page of Reddit. It kind of died down a bit, but then after a month or two it really started to grow into what it is today.

WHEN DID PEOPLE START RECOGN-IZING YOU?

t took a couple of months. I guess I really realized how big it was getting when I started getting asked to events, and to do appearances. That's when it kicked in, 'Oh, this is a real thing.'

ARE YOU STILL FRIENDS WITH IAN?

Oh yeah. He's my business partner

with all the stuff we do today with licensing and commercials. He's still very much involved with the Bad Luck Brian thing.

HOW HAVE YOU COPED WITH THE ATTENTION?

Ah, great! I know a decent amount of memes and a lot of them are like 'Oh it's terrible that this happened people used my image without permission.' Which is silly, because the more you resist, the more it's going to happen. It's one of the best things that's ever happened to me. You get the best parts of being famous where you get paid to do events and commercials and stuff, but nobody recognizes you day to day. I have a normal life and it doesn't affect me at all, because I don't look like the picture. I will tell people, 'Oh, that's me', and they'll literally say, 'No it's not'. People don't even believe me.

DO YOU ACTUALLY HAVE BAD LUCK?

I would say I have very good luck. In my lifetime I have won a decent amount of prizes. I've won an Xbox, a PSP, I've won so many giveaways and raffles.

WHY ARE PEOPLE DRAWN TO BRIAN?

The meme was created on the early side of memes – by which I mean the typical character memes such as Scumbag Steve or Overly Attached Girlfriend. People make memes about real life experiences, and at the time there were no memes that represented an unlucky personal experience. It was a funny-looking picture, but it also filled that void.

WHAT'S YOUR FAVOURITE BRIAN MEME?

One of my favourites is 'Parents get divorced, nobody fights over custody'. The first ones were a lot about Brian shitting his pants. They got more classy as it got bigger.

IS BRIAN JUST A JOKE, OR DO YOU THINK PEOPLE MAYBE SEE SOME OF THEMSELVES IN HIM?

I'm sure that's part of it. I think everybody relates to having bad luck, or something not going the way they wanted it to.

AGREED. I MEAN, WHO HASN'T SHIT THEMSELVES IN CLASS AT SOME POINT, AM I RIGHT? AHA!

UM, KYLE? YOU STILL THERE?? KYLE? BRIAN?? BRIAN??!!

END RECORDING.

CHAPTER 4

DICKS DICKS DICKS DICKS DICKS OUT

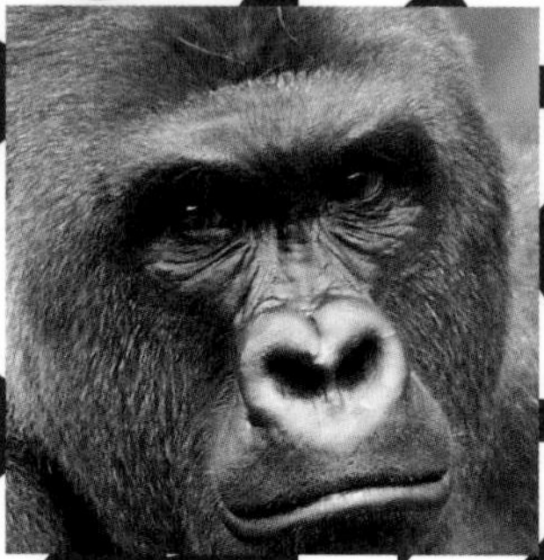

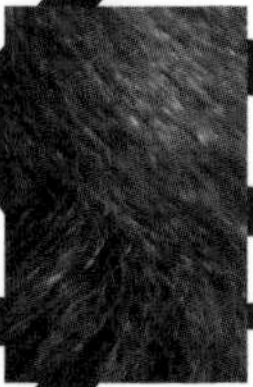

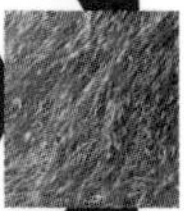

**THE STORY OF A FALLEN
GORILLA AND OTHER
ANIMALS WHO WON
THE HEARTS AND MINDS
OF A GENERATION**

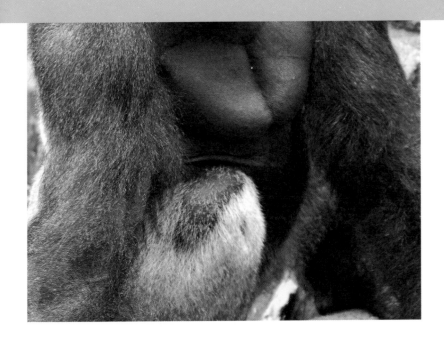

Anyway, enough of all this misery. I know what'll cheer you up. The same thing that cheers up every mopey sad-sack with next to no personality: animals!

The history of memes is peppered with the stories of pets and beasts who became internet sensations. Animals who grew from viral jokes into celebrities into brands, like Grumpy Cat or Doge. And they're big business. The scowling sadly-deceased feline Grumpy Cat's net worth

'WHAT HAPPENS TO AN ANIMAL WHEN IT IS ELEVATED INTO THE MEME KINGDOM?'

has been valued at $100 million (an amount her owner Tabatha Bundesen has disputed), and a parody cryptocurrency created in Doge's name is now reportedly worth a very real $1 billion.

But it isn't all about money. What about the lives of the animals who are thrust from the kennel into superstardom? What happens to an animal when it is elevated into the Meme Kingdom?

5 HILLARY AWARDS®
INCLUDING
BEST DIRECTOR 2016 · Donald J. Trump

UNOFFICIAL

A CLINTON FOUNDATION ASSASSINATION

Tom Harambe

saving private harambe

dicks out   30th august   never forget

★★★★★ "It's too bad there wasn't another way." Donald Trump

SPECIAL EDITION   DIRECTORS-CUT

JUSTICE FOR HARAMBE

In 2016 a three-year-old boy fell into the gorilla enclosure at Cincinnati Zoo: a fateful moment that resulted in one ape being shot to protect the child. In the days, weeks and months after his death at the hands of his keepers, Harambe the gorilla became a viral news story, then a folk hero, and then a meme.

The life and death of the Western lowland silverback gorilla who stole the hearts and minds of a generation is a tragedy with many lessons. It's a lesson in the meme cycle: how a genuinely tragic incident soon collapsed into an ironic, self-referential tailspin across the internet. It's a lesson in running a zoo, and the difficult decisions that arise when visitor safety and animal welfare come into conflict. But most of all it's a lesson in treasuring our loved ones, because we truly never know when they will be taken from us.

What makes a hero? Is it in their deeds? Their reputation? Or is it something more abstract than that? A sense, perhaps, that one being is greater, nobler, truer than the beasts they share the torn and dusty Earth with. This was true of Harambe the gorilla, a wise and gentle animal, whose untimely death sparked an online revolution. Using news reports, forum threads and a few educated guesses, we've pieced together a timeline of his formative and final moments.

Justice for Harambe
Dicks out for Harambe

THE DAILY MEME

OUR FALLEN HERO

GOOD NIGHT SWEET PRIN

FIG.7 HARAMBE'S STORY

THE LIFE OF HARAMBE

CIRCA 1999

The great and noble gorilla Harambe is born in captivity in a zoo in Texas.

SOME TIME IN 2014

Harambe is transferred to Cincinnati Zoo.

28 MAY 2016, 6:15AM

Harambe rises with the sun. He enjoys a mixture of stems and old fruits from the previous day, relishing the peace of his enclosure before the morning rush. 'How gentle sits the breeze,' he thinks to himself. Or something like that.

10:00AM

The zoo gates open. Harambe anticipates the clatter of feet, the churn of pushchair wheels and screams of childlike wonder he has known all his life. Helium balloons bounce on strings and the waft of candied nuts dances on the air.

12:00PM

Harambe sits in silence with his neighbouring gorillas as the lunchtime rush builds. He listens to the visitors' excited chatter, observes the extension of their selfie sticks, and contemplates the charming futility of their vanity.

1:14PM

Harambe eats a big stick and has a nap.

3:52PM

Cincinnati police receive a call that a baby has fallen into the moat around the gorilla enclosure. The child is identified as a three-year-old boy.

3 YEARS OLD

3:54PM

Reports begin to come in that Harambe has approached the boy. The zoo is heaving with thousands of visitors, many of whom begin to crowd around the enclosure, screaming or stunned in disbelief.

3:55PM

Harambe enters the water where the boy has fallen, takes him by the ankle and begins to swish him forwards and backwards. This moment is captured in footage that is shared extensively across the internet as events are unfolding. While reports from the fire service, who arrived later, suggest Harambe was trying to hurt him, most witnesses agree he seemed curious rather than violent. Nevertheless, panic is understandably growing as the 400-pound gorilla carries the boy further upstream.

3:56PM

Police callers report that Harambe is swinging the child back and forth on top of a rocky outcrop within the enclosure. Things are getting a bit tense.

4:00PM

Initial plans to tranquillize Harambe are dismissed as too dangerous, following fears that in the time it takes the sedative to take effect, the disorientated gorilla might lash out and endanger the boy further. The decision is therefore taken to shoot Harambe dead with a rifle. Zoo staff allow firefighters into the enclosure. They retrieve the child, who is then rushed to hospital.

29 MAY 2016

The boy's family release a statement to say he is 'doing just fine'. Yet online, the mood is souring. A Change.org petition is created calling on the authorities to hold the 'negligent' parents of the child responsible for Harambe's death.

31 MAY 2016

Republican presidential candidate Donald Trump is asked about the killing of Harambe in a press conference. Trump responds: 'It was amazing because there were moments with the gorilla – the way he held that child, it was almost like a mother holding a baby. Looked so beautiful and calm. And there were moments where it looked pretty dangerous.' Ultimately, he concluded, the zookeepers had no choice but to shoot him. 'It's too bad there wasn't another way.'

3 JUNE 2016

Muhammad Ali dies. Somebody mocks up an image of Harambe being KO'd by the legendary boxer, with the caption 'Muhammad Ali's first day in heaven'.

7 JUNE 2016

Twitter accounts, including WorldStarHipHop, tweet heavenly tableau of a cast of celebrity angels, adding Harambe to the list of high-profile deaths that have occurred in 2016 (David Bowie, Prince, Alan Rickman). They spread across Twitter faster than you can say, 'Harambe watches over us all'.

HARAMBE ☑

4 JULY 2016

Comedian Brandon Wardell coins the phrase 'Dicks out for Harambe' in a single, earth-shattering tweet.

5 JULY 2016

A Change.org petition is created, addressed to God, campaigning for Harambe to be brought back to life.

6 JULY 2016
Wardell posts a vine of him and the actor Danny Trejo repeating the phrase 'Dicks out for Harambe'.

9 JULY 2016
Reddit page r/dicksoutforharambe is launched.

10 JULY 2016
Three Ohio teenagers trick Google Maps into renaming the street their high-school is on as Harambe Drive.

23 JULY 2016
User @PrayForPatrick uses a Photoshopped image to trick Twitter into thinking Bernie Sanders has a framed photograph of Harambe in his living room.

9 AUGUST 2016
A Change.org petition is created, campaigning for the city of Cincinnati to be renamed 'the Kingdom of Harambe'.

16 AUGUST 2016
Polling reveals Harambe would receive 2% of the vote in Texas, were he in the presidential race against Donald Trump and Hillary Clinton.

20 AUGUST 2016
The Twitter account of Thane Maynard, director of Cincinnati Zoo, is hacked. He tweets the hashtag '#DicksOutForHarambe'.

22 AUGUST 2016
Thane Maynard tells Associated Press he is 'not amused' by the memes created in Harambe's name.

26 AUGUST 2016
Rapper Young Thug releases a mixtape called *Jeffrey*, featuring a track titled 'Harambe'.

8 NOVEMBER 2016
A false rumour spreads across the internet that Harambe received more than 11,000 votes in the US presidential election.

DICKS OUT FOR HARAMBE

31 DECEMBER 2016
The year of Harambe is over. With the gorilla's body long since dedicated to the Earth, a period of reflection is required for us to ask: what did it all mean? Why did Harambe the gorilla become a meme over any number of animals who are killed at the hands of humans every day? Many raise the point that there is a problematic, racist undertone to much of the Harambe-related humour, highlighting that the gorilla's image was part of the racist abuse also aimed at *Ghostbusters* star Leslie Jones. Others write it off as the ultimate expression of an age of meaninglessness – positioning Harambe as a post-ironic icon. Either way, his name is immortalized, an ape untethered from reality in a year of chaos.

6 FEBRUARY 2017
A Cheeto resembling Harambe is sold for $99,000 on eBay.

AND NOW A VERY SAD VISIT TO THE MEME PET CEMETERY

As is demonstrated with the demise of Harambe, death is not the end, especially if you're a 400-pound gorilla who becomes a meme, which I think we all are in our own way. With angel wings Photoshopped in place by bored teenagers and students, these images proved that it is possible for the life of a beloved animal to extend well beyond its short, earthly years. When a pet becomes a meme, it becomes something bigger, and that something can never die. The same has happened for a number of meme animals whose lives we remember today. Gone but never forgotten.

GABE THE DOG
(UNKNOWN–2016)

Gabe the Dog was an Eskimo-Pomeranian with a *voice*. Gabe rose to fame thanks to his distinctive bark, or 'bork', which YouTubers remixed to the tunes of popular songs, such as Toto's 'Africa' or Queen's 'Don't Stop Me Now'. His owner Jesse Hamel remembers him ...

We first got Gabe in January 2012. My mom had gone to the local animal rescue center (D'Arcy's ARC) because she wanted to walk dogs. Turns out Gabe had just gone up for adoption, and they were an instant match, so she ended up bringing him home that same day! Gabe was very peculiar. He had anxiety and separation issues, and in some ways was more cat-like than dog-like. He was very antisocial for the first couple of years, only tolerating the company of our family, but he gradually softened up and learned to love attention from others. He could be moody at times, but often did enjoy playing or getting belly rubs. He was happiest with all of our family around him, especially when we had our attention on him!

I had been making stuff on YouTube with a bunch of my friends for years, and it was mostly a very insular community – I only ever made stuff to amuse myself and my group of friends. When I started uploading clips of Gabe to my channel, my friends and I all started re-mixing the barks into various songs. Some of them got pretty popular,

'I THINK GABE WILL ALWAYS LIVE ON THROUGH THE MEMES.'

and before long I had a much bigger audience than I knew what to do with. I started uploading stuff more frequently, and things really took off when I started the Facebook page. I'm currently looking at my YouTube silver play button I received for breaking 100,000 subscribers and I still can't really believe it.

I think Gabe will always live on through the memes. I'm so proud of what we created – so many people used their creativity to make amazing stuff using Gabe's likeness and distinctive bark, and I think that creativity is what made him unique. To me, though, all of the internet stuff was secondary. He was just my weird little dog and I loved him. I'll remember his quirks, his weird bark, his soft puffy fur, and his personality – how he overcame his anxieties and learned to fit in with a family. I'm glad we gave him love and comfort, even for a short while. Everyone deserves that.

KEYBOARD CAT*

(DIED ONCE IN 1987, THEN AGAIN IN 2018)

THE 'HELLO? YES, THIS IS DOG' DOG

(DATES UNKNOWN)

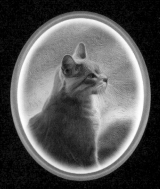

Keyboard Cat, real name Fatso, belonged to film-maker Charlie Schmidt, who filmed the original grainy clip of his cat playing an electric keyboard in 1984. Fatso sadly passed away in 1987, but was replaced by Bento, a similar ginger cat who took up the keyboard in 2007, sort of like when they changed the actor who played Aunt Viv in *The Fresh Prince* and hoped none of us would notice.

This dog, from a Serbian movie that came out in 1984, was popularized in the form of a screen grab of the mutt looking startled with a telephone against his ear. It proved pretty hard to track down the dog from a Serbian film from the 1980s. Surely dead, right? It would be the oldest dog in the world if it was still alive. Knowing my luck, he or she will be alive and will end up reading this book and I'll get a 'Hello, yes, this is the oldest dog in the world' email out of the blue.

*The cat pictured is Boots, not Fatso, who hopes one day to be as good on the keyboard as Fatso.

CECIL
THE LION

(2002–2015)

ACTUAL ADVICE
MALLARD

(2006–2014)

Cecil was a beloved lion who was found murdered and decapitated on the outskirts of Hwange National Park in Zimbabwe. Public outpourings of grief were fierce, and it wasn't long before the hunter who killed him was named as Walter James Palmer, a dentist from Minnesota. As was the case with Harambe, sincerity and sadness soon became irony and hyperbole, as meme-makers rinsed an over-sentimental public for suddenly caring about a lion they'd never heard of a week before. By the time of Harambe's death, weird Twitter users were mocking up images of Cecil the Lion battling the gorilla in animal heaven. Classy guys.

The Actual Advice Mallard was a duck who gave really fucking good advice. It's as simple as that! Hang your shirt up while you're in the shower so you steam it flat! Put a blue ink cartridge in a red pen so nobody steals it! You can heal paper cuts using a ChapStick! The actual duck in the stock image that was used for the meme was sadly killed in a wake-boarding accident while holidaying in Malibu three years ago. We reached out to the Actual Advice Mallard's family for comment, but they sadly couldn't respond as they are all ducks, you idiot.

CHAPTER 5

INTO THE DMS DMS DMS DMS

SEX AND LOVE IN THE
WORLD OF MEMES

For as long as there has been an internet, there have been people trying to get their end away on it. Unlike the fleshy confines of real-world dating, however, apps and websites have made things anonymous, global, fast-paced and instant. You can be the best version of yourself: a hunky Frankenstein's monster comprised of that one good photo of you from six years ago, an enhanced job title you don't actually use at work, and some funny chat-up lines you just mined from Reddit. You can also articulate every stage of your romantic trials through memes. Wahey!

'MEMES ARE NOW PRESENT AT EVERY STAGE OF THE LOVE CYCLE.'

As memes have gone mainstream, they've been put to use as a form of flirtation and even romance. Whether it's striking up a winking conversation on Tinder, or telling your husband how much he means to you, memes are now present at every stage of the love cycle. Then there are the memes for the 'forever alone', macros that do the job of articulating the desperation and devastation that comes with a broken heart. If you fancy it, we'd love to take you on a romantic twilight stroll through a few instances of the powerful effect memes have had on the world of dating and relationships. Call us!

WHEN YOU SEE SOME FINE ASS ANKLE

"DISREGARD FEMALES,
ACQUIRE CURRENCY."

JOSEPH DUCREAX – 1745

DISTRACTED BOYFRIEND: THE GREAT MEME LOVE TRIANGLE

Let's start with a love story.

Once upon a time there was a photographer called Antonio Guillem. Antonio wanted to tell the world a story, a story about a disloyal man with his girlfriend looking at another girl. So he hired three models, took a photograph of them and uploaded it to a stock image library. He called it: 'Disloyal man with his girlfriend looking at another girl'.

If there's one image that should spring to mind when the words 'meme' and 'relationships' are plonked next to each other, it's the Distracted Boyfriend. It's the most effective example of an 'object labelling' meme, a format that gained in popularity during the mid-2010s. Object labelling memes repurposing the meaning of a photo, by applying text boxes to different actors or objects in the image. In the case of Antonio's love triangle, the boyfriend was labelled to reflect any number of players who had been tempted away from the status quo by the promise of something new.

In 2017 the Distracted Boyfriend meme spread across the world with the pace and ferocity of herpes, with adaptations covering every topic from Phil Collins' turn from prog rock to pop music, to the plot of the first *Toy Story* movie. It wasn't long before the internet, along with major newspapers, started a hunt to find the people involved in creating the meme-world's first soap opera. Eventually, Antonio was tracked down and interviewed, only for him to claim that despite the fuss, he'd actually had no idea what a meme was until one of the models in the photo alerted him to the one he'd birthed.

As for the Distracted Boyfriend himself, the model known as Mario claims he is nothing like his character, telling *New York* magazine he would 'never look at someone like that in real life'. Nevertheless, his iconic saucy pout has become the perfect stand-in for the flitting attention spans of the internet age. He is the youth being led astray from capitalism by socialism, Trump's eyes wandering from being a normal president by Twitter, anyone who has been kept from sleep by thinking about sleep, or simply you being distracted from reading a real book by reading one about memes.

CLASSIFIED ADS

OOD FEMALE

best intentions but
out of context and
bolic of something
st touch with Andy
been feeling pretty
d of late.

character who has
ows how to have a
oking for someone
happy and see past
ned. If you think this
et in touch.

tact: P

WRITER SEEKS RELATIONSHIP

I've written an excellent book about memes, you might have read it.

Now it is time to share my experiences and create new ones!

NO NORMIES

Contact: AH

CONTACT: HT

I'M LOOKING FOR PEOPLE TO SEND ME EXPLICIT MEMES

45, FEMALE

I joined the meme world late and am looking for a young meme-lord to show me the ropes. Someone who can take me on e-quests and whisk me away to the darkest corners of the web.

Contact: TP

20, FEMALE
Contact: MM

goo.gl/2ACPsB

48, M, COLLECTOR

Here are some of my favourites. If you like what you see, get in touch.
Contact: GP

19, MALE
Looking for a woman who with a sense of humour, love to take walks, trade memes which we can enjoy together. Love holding hands and enjoying all that the web has to offer.
Contact: NG

FEISTY F4F
A feisty female looking to connect with other gamer-girls for good times.
Contact: DJ

I HAVE A

MEME COLLECTION WHICH IS QUITE BIG.

MASSIVE

EVEN: IT MAKES UP FOR MY TINY

DICK

Contact: SK

OOKING FOR HELP

u would call a 'normie'.
g for someone to open
nd heart to the world of
e danker the better. Do
a basement? Perfect!

Contact: NE

30, F, LONDON
Have struggled with indecision in the past. Often sat on the fence. Looking to right my wrongs and meet someone who I can share my online adventures with.
Contact: SM

MEME LOVER
If you don't know what this is don't bother getting in touch.

Contact: JR

30, M, LONDON
I love to run, particularly away from commitment (haha). When i'm not running I enjoy social-ising on chatrooms, posting to 4chan and memes which make me feel like a bad person.
Contact: SD

EXPERIENCED MALE
Experienced 20-something meme connoisseur interested in not only edgy but also spicy memes. Looking for a female with which to share valuable XP and talk at length about Harambe. Love taking photographs.
Contact: TP

FIG.8   CLASSIFIED ADS

DATING FOR NORMIES – A GUIDE TO LOVE, LOSS AND MEMES

We hear you've been a bit unlucky in love. (If by unlucky we mean 'deletes Tinder every Saturday, redownloads it every Sunday' and 'has a "usual" at Domino's Pizza'.) Whatever you do, you can't seem to get it right. You've tried it all – perfume, breath mints, botox, therapy – but nothing seems to work. Well, have you tried ... memes?

Hold on ... MEMES? You've connected this seemingly unrelated topic to ... memes? Yes, yes we have.

PLEASE CALL IF YOU NEED HELP WITH DATING. I WILL MINE YOUR HARD-DRIVE FOR INFORMATION WHICH WILL HELP YOU FIND YOUR TRUE LOVE.

CASH UP FRONT
NO REFUNDS

Can a meme actually get you laid? What sort of meme should you send a prospective lover? Is Spongebob ... sexy? Have no fear. We've been scouring the planet asking the loved up and lonely for their meme success stories and digital disasters, as well as collating the smoothest, cutest and downright filthiest memes in our archives, to produce the following instructional material on how memes can save your love life.

We guarantee this text will change your romantic fate, or, at the very least, give you something to read for the next couple of minutes. And that's a money-back guarantee!*

TURN OVER TO FIND OUT HOW!

1. MEMES ARE A MUST

If a bloke doesn't send me a meme, he's out. – Vicky, 22

The fact of the matter is, memes are a part of dating now. As online dating – through apps like Tinder, Bumble and Hinge – has become the predominant form of romantic socializing, hooking up has become inexorably intertwined with the language of the internet. If you're planning on using a dating app without at least a basic grasp of what a gif is, you might as well write them a letter with a portrait photograph of yourself enclosed

2. MAKE IT PERSONAL

If someone starts a conversation with a picture of a whale and the words 'WHALE HELLO', or a meme of some celeb taking a pair of sunglasses off, I'm off, because you probably send that to everyone and I've seen it before. If it's a really niche meme, then that might spark my interest, but if someone only talks in memes, that would jar with me. – Anna, 25

Where is it? Where is it? That's right, I've lost my libido thanks to that Drake meme you, and five other people, have sent me in the last twenty-four hours. Look, just because we said you need to send memes, that doesn't mean you can get away with sending the same crummy one as a conversation opener to everyone. You've still got to get to know the person – get a feel for their sense of humour, their interests. Only then should you send them that genuinely disturbing image of Thomas the Tank Engine you've got saved in your camera roll.

Hey, how you doin?

Yeah not bad

Kinda bored though, you?

Yeah not bad, about to go out, i'll talk to you later

Thursday 11:19 AM

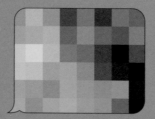

Was this meant for me?

Yeah, told you i'd send you funny stuff 🙂

The phone number you're trying to contact is no longer available.

Please contact your service provider or get better chat.

3. MEMES ARE NOT SEXY

4. ANIMALS

A guy once sent me a terrible meme that he genuinely thought was funny. I have no idea how he got the tone so wrong. It was basically a woman being f*cked by a guy while her breasts hit him in the face. Seriously, that was it. That was the joke. To give some context, we'd been on three dates and things had been going fairly well. I replied saying, 'Was this for me?' and he said, 'Yeah, told you I'd send funny stuff :).' With a smiley! After that I completely friend-zoned him. Totally killed the romance.
– Georgia, 25

While memes play a very important role in building up a rapport with someone, it is very difficult, if not completely impossible to translate that into the bedroom. Sure, crack out a few images of macros during your pre-match small talk, but once things start to get steamy, best to leave the trollface downstairs. If you're trying to suggest something freaky with a meme, you've probably misread some, if not all, signals. So, erm, yes, don't send pornographic memes to people you don't know very well. This is very important life advice.

Before me and my boyfriend were dating I went home to visit my family and see my dog. We were chatting and he kept sending me dog memes. Very fluffy, very safe. As someone who didn't know much about memes before that point, they were very accessible, and I think I liked the idea he was specifically seeking out dog content for me. – Rose, 21

If in doubt: animals. This is a golden rule of the internet, one that has particular resonance in the arena of internet dating. Send someone a heart-warming image of a dog and it barely matters what the joke on the meme is, they'll be powerless to resist! Unless the dog is dead.

5. PAY ATTENTION TO WHAT YOU RECEIVE

Whenever someone sends me a meme or a gif, it makes me realize whether we're on the same wavelength with regards to taste and sense of humour. How vulgar someone might be? How silly are they? But also whether or not they get me.
– Peter, 26

LUKEWARM MEMES

Don't just concentrate on what you're sending them; equally important is what you get back. You can tell a lot about a person from the memes they send! That heart-throb from work just sent you an image of Thanos clenching his Infinity Gauntlet? He may not have the requisite emotional maturity to participate in a functioning adult relationship. That cute girl from Tinder just sent you the Sean Bean 'One Does Not Simply ...' meme? She may be 45.

6. KEEP THINGS SPICY

Way back in a previous, single life, I had a strictly held belief that Shrek memes held the key to dating app success. It's unbearably squalid to type out now, but in the dark fag end of 2016 it felt like both the real and right thing to do. Just about 'online' enough to seem current, but not nerdy enough to feel entirely American Pie. At first, it sort of worked, when a few baffled responses turned into unsatisfactory dates. But it ran out of steam after around six months of swiping. I've no idea why that was – though I imagine it had something to do with losing faith in the schtick itself, and the pretty dreadful quality of dates it provoked. – Chris, 23

For goodness sake: take a risk! You didn't get this far in life posting lukewarm Success Kid memes, you miserable pipsqueak. Be yourself! Roll the dice! Try that incomprehensible Galaxy Brain you picked up in the back-reaches of 4Chan, or take a punt on something from your 'too hot for Tumblr' Marxist meme-stash. If they don't love you at your spiciest, they don't deserve you at your niciest!

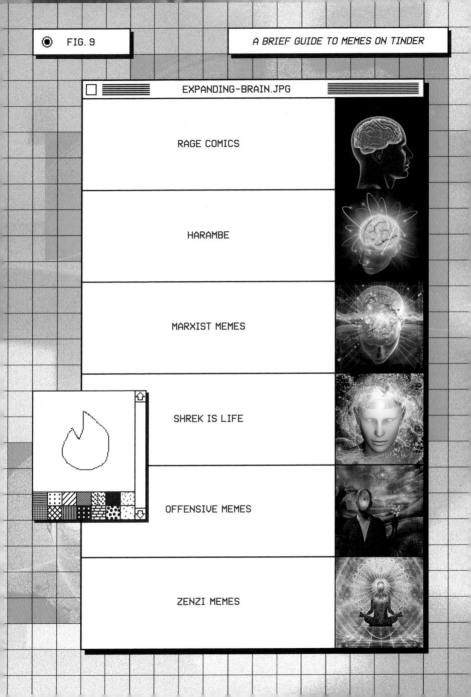

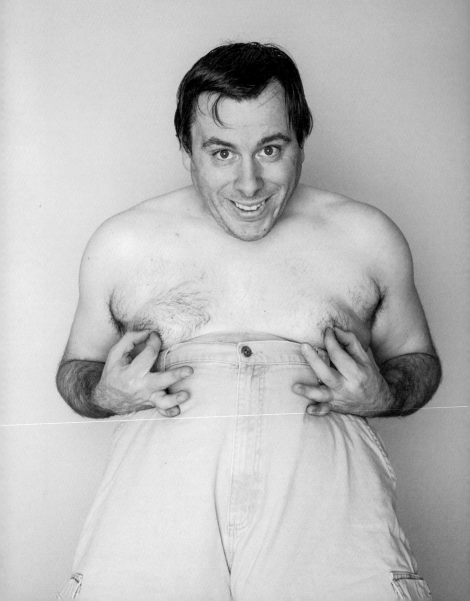

My girlfriend and I always try to send one meme to each other every time we log onto Instagram. Most of the memes we send are relationship-oriented, and it's just one of many ways we convey love to each other. Essentially all we're doing is leaving little gifts to make the other one smile. It makes the bad days a little better and the good days amazing. – Declan, 17

My ex-girlfriend definitely sent me a meme of that old woman from Titanic – 'It's been 84 years' – when we hadn't had sex for a while. Funny, isn't it? Well, that relationship wasn't, but we got a good meme out of it and as a millennial that's all you can ask for. – Harry, 24

MEMES > ISSUES

So, you're going steady now, but that doesn't mean you should switch off the charm. It's important to pay attention to your significant other, and what better way to do that than with memes, the modern-day Hallmark card. Struggling to say 'I love you'? Don't worry, there's a meme for that! Sorry seems to be the hardest word? There's a meme for that too! Looking to propose an open relationship in a way that's tactful but also alluring? I mean, there likely isn't a meme for that, but a picture of Salt Bae will probably take the edge off.

Just as you can tell how great things are going from the memes you're sending to each other, they are also a pretty good indicator of if, and when, things are taking a nosedive. When the content you're sharing turns to passive-aggressive hints, bleak 'Me IRL' memes and an endless slew of Overly Attached Girlfriend macros, the jig is up. When the memes have turned stale, read the signs and call it off, or risk walking in on your one and only exchanging *Simpsons* screengrabs with somebody new.

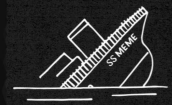

SS MEME

*I'd honestly love to see you try and pull this off. Go on mate, try and get your money back. Try. How would you even go about it? Small claims court? Hire a solicitor? Bollocks would you. You wouldn't know where to start! Amateur

WHY FAILS, F*CK-UPS AND SCHADENFREUDE ARE THE BACKBONE OF INTERNET LULZ

Not to sound like your parents but, hey, everybody fails. It's a universal experience shared by all humans. We are united in our screw-ups, our mistakes, our embarrassment and disappointment. If memes are all about communicating ideas, then it should come as no surprise that fucking up is one of the most common themes.

It's unclear when exactly 'FAIL' entered the online vocabulary, but as a piece of internet slang, it's been used to describe everything from missed penalties to acts of war. Unlike many of the other memes we've met so far in our journey, fail memes are about a term rather than a character or an image. Since the beginning of memes, people have been slapping the word on pictures of upturned trucks, faceplants and dodgy Photoshops. Depressingly, we enjoy looking at images of other people's mistakes and misfortunes so much that their popularity as a genre has barely dipped in over a decade.

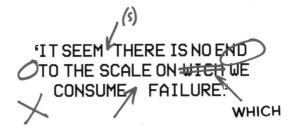

'IT SEEM~~S~~ THERE IS NO END TO THE SCALE ON ~~WICH~~ WE CONSUME FAILURE.'

WHICH

If anything, the FAIL industry has become bigger. In 2008 the Cheezburger Network – a meme-media empire founded by online entrepreneur Ben Huh – launched FAILBlog, a sort of nerve centre for all things fail. Screw-up archivists FailArmy have perhaps found the most success. At the time of writing, their Facebook page has 17 million likes, their YouTube channel 14 million subscribers, and they even had their own syndicated TV series. It seems there is no end to the scale on which we will consume failure. We want faster slides into disrepute, harder falls from bicycles, and more precise collisions with glass doors people didn't know were there because they were so clean.

Who would have guessed it? People are cruel.   **PLEASE SEE ME!**

A TALE OF TWO FAILS

As an exercise in the universality of online failure, let us pick apart two choice examples. The nation: America. Two men, separated by status and notoriety, but united by just how voraciously the internet gobbled up their mistakes.

The first of these men is called Dunta Pickett. It was the summer of 2016. To celebrate his birthday, Dunta had cooked himself a delicious, grisly-looking rack of ribs surrounded by all the trimmings. It was his special day and he was sparing no expense! In an effort to share his meal with the world, he took a photograph of it and uploaded it to Facebook with the caption: 'My BIRTHDAY dinner to myself...bone Apple tea.'

It was a simple mistake, sort of. Clearly, having heard the French phrase *bon appétit*, meaning 'enjoy your meal', Dunta had confused it for the slightly less well-known phrase 'bone apple tea', meaning, well, who knows?

The internet being, well, the internet, it wasn't long before 'bone apple tea' was everywhere. A screenshot of the post was shared on a Subreddit called r/SadCringe (which feels a bit mean) and the phrase was being included in 'Idiots of the Internet' compilations. Shortly after this, Twitter users began posting pictures of food with the caption 'bone app the teeth'. When Dunta finally saw that his mistake had spread like wildfire, he took it in good faith, commenting, 'Don't get in your feeling cause I'm going viral!'

MY

BIRTHDAY DINNER TO MYSELF...

The second of these men is the current President of the United States: Donald Trump.

On 30 May 2017, Trump, an avid Twitter user (in case you hadn't noticed), tweeted the following statement: *Despite the constant negative press covfefe.*

Like, just that. Covfefe. He just said covfefe and then left it hanging. Everyone, everywhere scratched their heads in unison. U wot m8? Covfefe? What does covfefe mean? Is it a word now? What does it mean in Russian? Is that what Bill Murray was whispering in Scarlett Johansson's ear at the end of *Lost in Translation*? Newspapers dedicated column inches to it, online dictionaries set about trying to define it, I tried to order a tube of it from my chemist, the world slipped and spun away from its axis.

'DESPITE THE CONSTANT NEGATIVE PRESS COVFEFE.'

Then the following morning it was deleted, and replaced by another tweet in which Trump asked, 'Who can figure out the true meaning of "covfefe"???' before imploring us to 'Enjoy!' After all that, it was simply the mother of all typos – and a fail the world will never forget.

So you see ... it doesn't matter if you're an anonymous bloke photographing your birthday dinner, or the leader of the free world: the internet never forgets.

THE DAILY MEME
— FAIL DICTIONARY —

EPIC FAIL

Sometimes 'FAIL' just won't cut it. Some fails are bigger. Some fails are massive. Some fails there is no coming back from. Some fails are *epic*. The sort of phrase that makes you want to break somebody's jaw!

DERP

Use this expression whenever you hear someone saying something stupid. For example:

You: The last book I read before this was the instruction manual for my vape.
Me: Derp.
You: I enjoyed it better tbh.

YOU HAD ONE JOB

This popular internet expression usually accompanies pictures or images where people have managed to fail monumentally at a simple, straightforward task. Like the person who checked the spelling throughout this book.

OWNED/ PWNED

Originally from the world of gaming, if somebody owns you, or pwns you (to use the correct terminology), then you have had failure served to you. You've been humiliated, dominated and crushed. Checkmate. Game over. Put the book down and walk away.

RARE PET

WIN

WINNING

The opposite of a FAIL. Charlie Sheen's favourite pastime.

COVFEFE

DONALD IS THAT YOU?

3D SET DESIGN
PROPS
3D MEMES

CONTACT:
ANTON

RARE TO SHEKEL
CONVERSION

FROG AN
CONTR

But as one dog-whistle for co
one's a new low. Whenever some
shows up in the replies to point o
is widely regarded as a popular
meme, a flood of other frog-adve
accounts chime in to scream tha

RARE MEME
CARETAKER
UNCOVERED

Rare meme caretaker only ju
Alex Cox revealed today that
last eight years working for th
Russian Meme Intelligence a
was paid to do a job which I
shouldn't be judged for. Eve
I did was for my family and
make a living. My speciality
Rares and spicy memes. I
very good at my job.

POST-P
~~DEPRES~~
SUPPO

CONTA
RICH.

SCHADENFREUDE

Schadenfreude is an emotion defined simply as 'taking pleasure in the misfortune of others'. It's something we all experience day to day. The glee as your younger brother's *Brazzers* subscription comes up on your dad's credit card bill, the thrill as your 'cool skateboard friend' becomes your 'less cool on the floor friend with a broken ankle' friend. Hell, I'm experiencing it right now, watching you try to pronounce schadenfreude over and over again in your head.

It doesn't take a genius to work out that FAIL memes are a basic continuation of this emotional tradition. Tiffany Watt-Smith is a research fellow at the Centre for the History of Emotions at Queen Mary University in London. She's written a whole book about schadenfreude, so I called her up to ask how enjoying fails has changed our behaviour.

WHAT DOES THE CENTRE FOR THE HISTORY OF EMOTIONS DO?

We look at the changing meanings attached to emotions, how different emotional words have changed over time, and the way different emotional cultures move around over time. And one of the things we look at a lot is how certain emotions come in and out of fashion at different times. Schadenfreude is an emotion that is in fashion at the moment. That's why I was interested to work on it.

HOW OLD IS SCHADENFREUDE AS AN IDEA?

Well, it's a German word that came into the English language in the middle of the nineteenth century, but it's really in the last twenty years you start noticing it more. It seems to be a concept we've become quite interested in recently. I think this is to do with the internet primarily, actually, to do with Twitter pile-ons and the way we treat celebrities. An anxiety that perhaps we've become crueller.

DICKHEAD

HOW CONSISTENT IS SCHADENFREUDE THROUGHOUT HUMAN HISTORY?

It's a very consistent thing and it's consistently worried about as well. In most philosophical cultures and most medical cultures you've got someone saying 'I'm worried about this, we shouldn't be doing it', and giving it a bad rap. Most philosophers through the ages think schadenfreude is not a pleasant part of human behaviour.

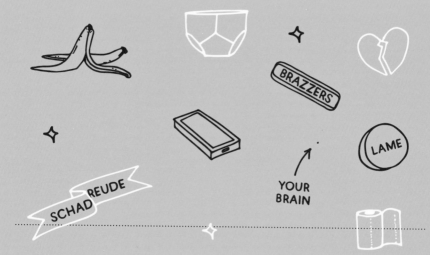

SCHADREUDE

YOUR BRAIN

LAME

BRAZZERS

'THE THRILL AS YOUR "COOL SKATEBOARD FRIEND" BECOMES YOUR "LESS COOL ON THE FLOOR FRIEND WITH A BROKEN ANKLE".'

STUPID

SAD

HALF EMPTY

RETURN

TO SENDER

SHIT   SHOES

PLZ STOP

FIG.11   *THE SCHADENSCALE*

STEP RIGHT UP LADIES AND GENTLEMEN, BOYS AND GIRLS,
RATE YOURSELF ON THE SCHADENSCALE. ARE YOU A
SPITEFUL, HORRIBLE HUMAN BEING OR COULD YOU BE OUR
SAVIOUR? FIND OUT TODAY!

YOU ARE MOTHER TERESA

YOU STILL HAVE DIAL-UP INTERNET

YOU THINK A MEME IS A POKEMON

YOU ARE A REGULAR HUMAN BEING

FAIL VIDEOS ARE YOUR LIFEBLOOD

YOU TORMENT YOUR PET FOR LIKES

YOU'RE A SICK BASTARD, YOU KNOW THAT?

DONALD, IS THAT YOU?

YOU WILL BURN IN HELL

REGULAR 4CHAN USER

HAS THE INTERNET CHANGED HOW WE EXPERIENCE SCHADENFREUDE?

Well, schadenfreude describes taking pleasure in others' misfortunes but it's a spectator sport. It's not about enjoying inflicting pain on someone else. In relation to the internet I think that distinction gets quite blurry. If you're enjoying a politician looking idiotic and someone's made a meme of them and you share that, then you're part of the pile-on. You're both enjoying the misfortune and contributing to the humiliation of that person. I think memes complicate the usual defence of schadenfreude, which is: 'Well, I'm enjoying but I've got nothing to do with it, it's not my fault.'

SO WHAT DO YOU THINK? ARE MEMES MAKING US CRUELLER?

Well, I'm a historian, and I look at the history of emotions, and one of the things that I see is that people often have these moments where they worry they're living in an age of some emotion. For the Victorians it was boredom, because they were really invested in productivity. I think we're worried about schadenfreude these days because we've become incredibly invested in empathy as a concept. There has been a lot of money and research put into empathy, and teaching it in schools. In the context of valuing empathy, schadenfreude looks really weird and perverse, when actually it's completely normal and silly most of the time.

SO, ME ENJOYING TWENTY-MINUTE-LONG 'SKATEBOARD FAIL' VIDEOS IN MY PANTS ISN'T NECESSARILY A NEW HUMAN EXPERIENCE?

Schadenfreude has always been shared. There's an Egyptian tombstone from, I think, the fourth century BC, that's got a picture of a craftsman dropping a mallet on his foot and the people around him laughing at him. It's not that this is an invention of our time. These images have been shared in public, commemorated on tombstones, for a long time.

WHY DO WE ENJOY WATCHING OTHER PEOPLE FAIL?

There are lots of reasons. One of them is justice. We enjoy seeing someone we think deserves it getting their comeuppance. You can see that in a lot of those fail videos. Let's say it's a TV presenter who is acting all grown-up and then gets attacked by wasps or something. It makes them look silly when they're trying to look important. Politicians are often in that situation. Or someone trying to do a really impressive wheelie on a bike and not managing it. There's an enjoyment to over-reaches.

HAS HIDING BEHIND A COMPUTER SCREEN MADE THAT ENJOYMENT EASIER?

If I see someone barge past an old lady at a zebra crossing, and I say 'Hey, don't do that. Didn't you see that woman?', that's a big thing for me to do. I risk being punched, shouted at, or socially humiliated in some other way. It's not easy. On the internet, though, it's incredibly easy. There's no risk of retaliation. Also on the internet there's already an audience, and scientists have found people are much more likely to punish transgressors when there's an audience.

THIS IS PROBABLY A STUPID QUESTION, BUT WHY DO YOU THINK WE ENJOY WATCHING SOMEONE LIKE DONALD TRUMP FUCK UP?

I think politicians failing in general is glee-inducing. Because Trump is shooting from the hip and constantly on Twitter he opens himself up to many opportunities for screwing up. I remember in the run-up to the most recent election, there was a lot of hand-wringing about schadenfreude. Democrats were rubbing their hands with glee at Trump's stupidity but actually they weren't noticing what he was really doing and how powerful he was becoming. He's not the idiot you think he is. So schadenfreude was a dangerous distraction in that case.

THIS IS PROBABLY AN EVEN STUPIDER QUESTION, BUT IF SCHADENFREUDE IS ALL ABOUT ENVY OR JUSTICE, WHY DO WE ENJOY WATCHING VIDEOS OF DOGS FAILING?

In my little categories of schadenfreude, there's justice, but there's another part of it which is recognizing that we all fail. We all screw up and we all feel ourselves failing all the time. We never quite do things the way we want to do them, no one does. Perhaps some of the pleasure, when we see a dog failing is feeling part of a community of failure. It releases some of the burden of having to be perfect or do well. We see failure around us, and see it as something important, something to be embraced. It feels like a relief. I also think part of why we enjoy accidents – silly, daft ones – is because they connect us to the absurdity of the world and the futility of our attempts to remain in control of it. There's probably something that connects dogs running into windows with Samuel Beckett.

SO, I'M NOT TOTALLY EVIL?

To me, schadenfreude isn't great, obviously. It would probably be better if we didn't feel it, but we do. It tells us when we're feeling inferior, powerless or in competition, so it's useful. But also it is, ultimately, a counter to the culture of perfection we find ourselves living in. Sometimes we even invite people to feel schadenfreude on our behalf. You go into a new social situation, a new job, everyone makes self-deprecating jokes because that's how you'll bond and not be seen as a threat. I think it's an important emotion that's unfairly maligned, that can be part of how we bond as well as laugh at each other.

STUPID
IDIOT
FOOL
TWAT
DUMB
ASS
KLUTZ

HA HA HA HA HA HA HA HA HA HA HA

HI! HI! HI! HI!

FIG.12   BIOMETRIC BRAIN SCAN: SPECIMEN 1A

AND NOW, LADIES AND GENTLEMEN, BOYS AND GIRLS. STEP RIGHT UP AND TAKE A BRIEF LOOK INSIDE MY MIND

→

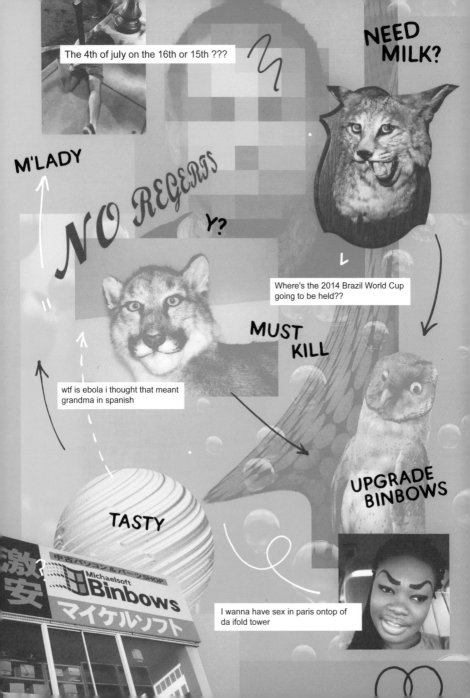

CHAPTER 7

MEME MEME MEME MEME MEME WARS

**MEET THE MANY TRIBES
OF THE MEME-IVERSE, AND
FIND OUT WHAT HAPPENS
WHEN THEY CLASH**

THE BIGGEST
DISAPPOINTMENT IS

YOU

Hopefully by now you've grasped that memes are only as good as their audience. That is to say: just because a joke doesn't make sense to you, that doesn't mean it isn't funny. For example, I could tell you a joke about my mate's dad Gordon. You won't find it funny because you don't know Gordon, but that doesn't mean it isn't funny at all. It's actually hilarious. Ask Gordon.

Like all languages, while memes started off in the same basic place, they have quickly developed and divided off into countless specific variations. Beyond normie memes, or memes that evoke the universality of human failure, there's a whole world of image macros so specific, so unbelievably minute in their reach, you'll barely believe they exist in the first place. These are memes only big enough for small groups, single professions, specialist subjects and, in some cases, one joke. There are memes for everything: garlic bread, moths, Marxism and everything in between.

A BEGINNER'S GUIDE TO THE WORLD
OF WEIRD MEME COMMUNITIES

So without hesitation, let us consider some of the weirdest, nichest meme tribes in existence, the forums and fan-pages that rely so heavily on in-jokes they're practically agoraphobic.

TRUCK DRIVER MEMES

I HATE BEING SEXY BUT I'M A TRUCK DRIVER SO I CAN'T HELP IT …

WHAT?   Truck driver memes.
WHERE?   Private Facebook Group
PEOPLE? 1,896 members at time of writing.

Truck driver memes is your one-stop shop for relatable trucking laughs, and memes about big rigs and heavy loads. Know that sinking feeling when you haven't done your logs in two days and you spot a cop in your rear-view mirror? Ever seen another trucker and thought, 'Yup, his DF filters are going to be clogged in the morning!'? Then this is the group for you.

I created the group in 2016, aimed at having a community for truckers, and family and friends of truckers, to relate and share things with each other. Most members are Americans but a lot are African, Middle Eastern and Canadian. I have another meme group that focuses on everything memes. I try to integrate memes from trucking but they usually go over the heads of non-truckers. – Don Perkins, admin behind the group

VS

TREBUCHET MEMES

ALL HAIL THE SUPERIOR SIEGE ENGINE!

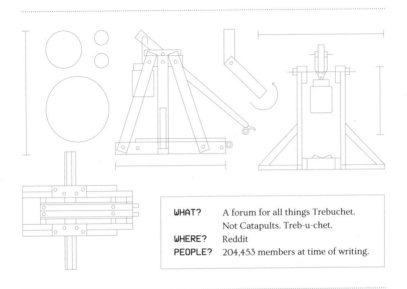

WHAT?	A forum for all things Trebuchet. Not Catapults. Treb-u-chet.
WHERE?	Reddit
PEOPLE?	204,453 members at time of writing.

One for the discerning military buffs who know a superior siege engine when they see it, this Reddit group is all about the ultimate counterweight weapon capable of throwing payloads of 90 kilograms up to 300 metres. Memes on the, actually very popular, Trebuchet Memes Subreddit celebrate this seminal destroyer of castles in every way imaginable. Just don't mention the c-word.

The memes are about trebuchets, and the humour comes from a satirical critique on the status quo. Something like a trebuchet is so insignificant to anyone in their daily lives that the absurdity of any one user's obsession is funny, let alone 200 thousand people. The trebuchet itself forms a rallying point from which the absurdity can take place. The community here is very tight-knit. We do very little moderation because the community does a good job of self-moderating. The fact that the sub is so large and active is a joke in itself because it is such a niche topic. If looking at memes about trebuchets improves your day even the slightest bit, then I think that is why we are here: it's to make people happy. – u/willbobchil0n

BELLRINGING MEMES

'WHEN THE CONDUCTOR CALLS A SINGLE ... BUT YOU RING A BOB.'

WHAT? Memes all about the intricacies, ups and downs of the ancient art of bellringing.

WHERE? Facebook page

PEOPLE? 721 members at time of writing.

Far from the clanging chimes of doom, it turns out the world of bell-ringing is actually hilarious! Well, if you know what the word 'Grandsire' means. Or 'bob'. Or 'change-ring-ing'. Or if you know what 'Stedman Cinques' are. Look, forget it, just know that the next time you walk past a church with a tower, or hear bells echoing through the streets on a Sunday morning, somebody, some-where, is probably pissing them-selves laughing.

The English tradition of bellringing is very old, and, like many old Eng-lish traditions, tends to involve a fair amount of going to the pub in addi-tion to the activity itself. Naturally, it was in a pub after a few rounds that I and a few of my fellow university ringers had the thought to make a bellringing memes group. This was in 2012, I believe ... In general, meme formats can be successful for varying reasons, but one I see a lot is 'obser-vational comedy'-type memes that make people go 'Oh yeah, that hap-pens all the time'. When you have a niche hobby, those formats fit very well. As I see it, memes are like all forms of in-joke, where understand-ing the humour acts as a natural test of belonging to a community, be that for better or worse. – Vic Smith, group admin.

MARINE SCIENCE MEMES FOR TELEOST TEENS

WHAT?   Marine science memes, duh.
WHERE?   Facebook page
PEOPLE? 2,667 likes at time of writing.

It's safe to say that the study of ocean-ography and marine biology hasn't always walked hand in hand with Big Laughs, but that's all changed now. This page puts the *rofl* in *marine microflora*. Laugh-out-loud-funny memes that cover everything from coral erosion to that awkward feeling when you're a conservationist and someone brings up how many fish you kill for data.

I'm a University of New South Wales (Australia) honours student, and I started marine science memes about a year ago. It started as a joke as a few friends and I were complaining about there being no marine science meme pages, but now there are a few, I think. They're usually reflective of ironic situations or ideas that spring to mind from uni classes/research in the past. They're all broadly related to marine science or fisheries science, as that is my field of focus. – Marine Science Memes, page admin

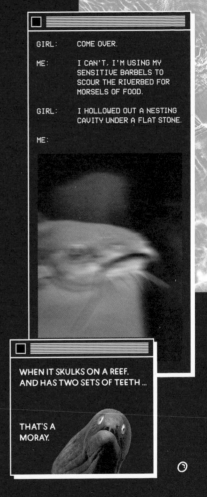

GIRL: COME OVER.

ME: I CAN'T, I'M USING MY SENSITIVE BARBELS TO SCOUR THE RIVERBED FOR MORSELS OF FOOD.

GIRL: I HOLLOWED OUT A NESTING CAVITY UNDER A FLAT STONE.

ME:

WHEN IT SKULKS ON A REEF. AND HAS TWO SETS OF TEETH ...

THAT'S A MORAY.

BOG MEMES

WHAT?   Bog memes. As in: memes
          about bogs. Peaty, muddy,
          Irish bogs.
WHERE?   Facebook page
PEOPLE?   Honestly, 74k at time of
          writing.

One of the most popular niche meme pages on Facebook composed exclusively of memes about — *checks notes* — bogs and the — *checks notes again, squints eyes* — experiences of people who plough them. Jokes aside, working the bog-cutting turf is a long-held tradition in rural Ireland, so perhaps it's no mistake that there are memes about peat-covered wetlands. Oh, and did you know that thanks to the particular chemical traits of the bog, objects found in them have often been preserved for thousands of years? So if nothing else, at least these memes should age well.

It's a one-person operation. I made a meme about the bog and put it on a friend's page, it got a few likes and he suggested I start a 'bog memes' page, so I did. The memes are about the bog and turf, it's an Irish way of life you could say. The humour comes from experience of the bog. There's community between the people who live in the countryside and then the people from urban areas who have no idea what the memes are about.
— Bog Memes, admin

WHEN YOU PRETEND TO BE POORLY SO YOU DON'T HAVE TO GO TO THE BOG

WHEN YOUR AULD PA ASKS YOU TO GO TO THE BOG

WHAT'S A MEME WAR, GRANDAD?

You kids today don't know anything. You haven't had to live through the horrors we have. The carnage. You see these scars: that's what three Meme Wars in two years'll do to you. Lost a lot of a good men in those struggles. Hard-fought things, Meme Wars. I still hear the sound of downvotes in my dreams. Falling onto me like acid rain. And those are the nights I can sleep. You wouldn't understand. You weren't there. You could never understand.

Sadly, when you have lots of communities vying for the same territory, it usually leads to only one thing: WAR. And in this respect, memes are no different. Meme Wars have been fought since the mid-2010s, and since then a series of conflicts have left the online landscape changed permanently.

'YOU WEREN'T THERE. YOU COULD NEVER UNDERSTAND'

The first instance of a full-blown Meme War is generally understood to have taken place in the lead-up to the election of Donald Trump as the 45th President of the United States, when online forces of the far right united to co-opt cartoon frogs and lead a charge of memes that sought to put their man in the White House. Yet since then, the term has come to refer to a different sort of online escapade. Beckett Mufson is a digital culture journalist who has written about Meme Wars from the frontline for *VICE*. He defines them, in theory, more as a sport than a real conflict. 'It's usually started by the mods of two consenting Subreddits, who build on a friendly rivalry to see who can muster up the most mass on their respective teams and take over each other's pages,' he explains.

WAR IS OVER

The casualties were many, the costs were high, the stakes so low. Find out more inside.

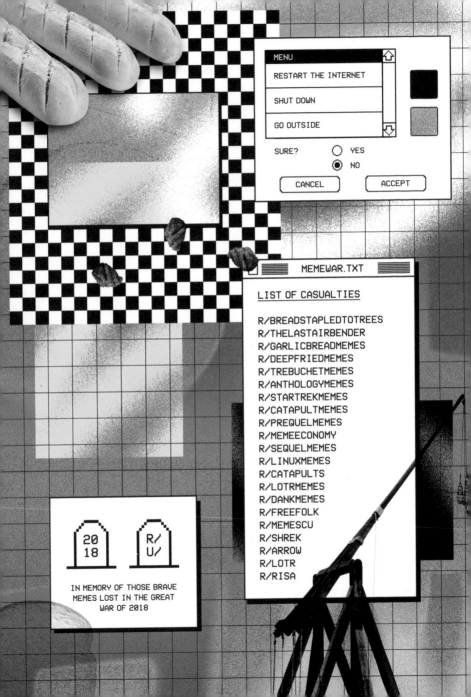

Reddit, if you haven't used it before, is a website that aggregates content and then ranks it based on 'upvotes' and 'downvotes'. Meme wars exploit these basic mechanics for competition – invading other Subreddits and posting unrelated content, or downvoting the existing content so it sinks out of sight. 'It might start out with a crossover meme posted by a member of both communities, and escalate from there', Beckett adds. 'It ends when there's a clear winner or it gets boring.'

In 2018, however, things got serious. The first-ever Meme World War began when a 'Star Wars Prequel Memes' Subreddit invaded a 'Star Wars Sequel Memes' Subreddit. Beckett remembers the conflict as different from the Meme Wars that came before it. 'It was HUGE,' he recalls. 'Decades of contempt and affection for the prequels, and the national conversation about whether the sequels were good or bad, made a rivalry between Prequel Memes and Sequel Memes a good story, which the other Subreddits were thrilled to be a part of.'

At the height of the conflict more than 150 Subreddits were pulled into the war, with the bulk of the damage being inflicted by an alliance between Prequel Memes, Trebuchet Memes and a Garlic Bread Memes Subreddit (among others). Soon the tone began to deteriorate. 'In less than a week, the spirit of the game was violated on multiple levels,' Beckett tells us. 'The war was ended when one of the moderators was doxxed – a serious act of aggression in the middle of a game.' Doxxing is the act of researching and revealing private information about somebody who is otherwise anonymous online. 'It's like if someone pulled a knife in a basketball game, or blackmailed you to win at Settlers of Catan.' The war ended after twelve days of fighting, bringing the biggest Meme War in Reddit's history to a close.

'There's a memorial Subreddit that posts every so often, reminiscing about the war like old veterans,' Beckett reports. 'Some people want to start a new one, but I don't know if we'll ever have one that big and fun again.' In the light of the Meme World War, many fear the period now entered into will resemble a Meme Cold War, as posters begin stockpiling content for the next conflict. For now, relative peace reigns across Reddit, but how long this can last is unclear.

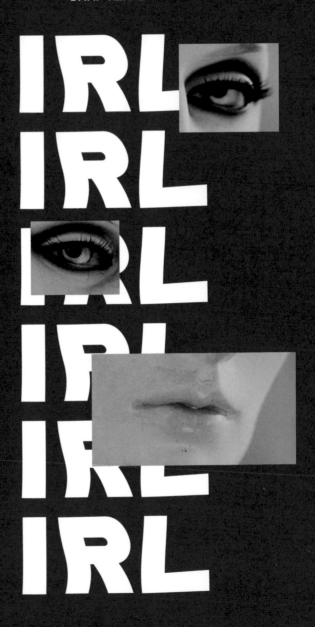

CHAPTER 8

IRL
IRL
IRL
IRL
IRL
IRL

WHAT HAPPENS WHEN MEMES CROSS OVER INTO THE REAL WORLD?

In the pre-meme world, it used to be said that life imitates art. Well, even though we've now done away with art and replaced it with memes, the same truth still stands. As the peoples of the world have gorged on internet gags and pointless videos, memes too have found their way through laptop lids and into the physical world. This has happened in obvious ways – yes, you can buy Grumpy Cat socks now; no, we don't want them for our birthday – but also in ways that are less direct. Not getting it? Okay, let's talk about planking ...

WHAT EXACTLY IS ... PLANKING?

The origins of planking are unclear. Most people agree it started in Australia – various people claim credit for having invented the term – where people were doing it as early as 2007, but it wasn't until 2011 that the craze really swept the world. It was simple enough: all you had to do was lie face-down, like a plank, in an unusual setting and have someone take your picture. People went nuts for it, sharing their planks far and wide. People planked on televisions, phone boxes, school desks, cars and live animals. Things quickly started to get out of hand: staff in an English hospital were suspended for planking during a shift, and not long after that an Australian man fell seven storeys to his death after planking on a balcony. Eventually the Australian prime minister was forced to make a statement about the fad, calling for plankers to consider their safety.

What's really interesting to us, though, is how planking caught on and spread. Just like a meme, it started with an idea that people took, created their own version of and then shared. Only this time, instead of downloading and editing pictures, people put themselves in the middle of the action. Planking was a bona fide, real-world meme.

THE DAILY MEME

PLANKING CRAZE SWEEPS THE NATION

Elliot Titterington

June 12th, 2017

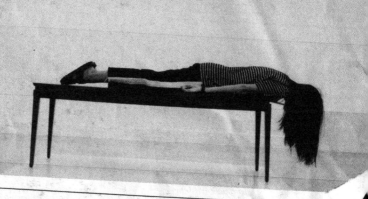

WALNUT WHIP IN CUSTODY OVER SEXUAL ASSAULT

FIG.14   PLANKING

THEN WHAT?

Since those heady, face-down-on-a-bus-stop days, there have been plenty of other real-world memes. Perhaps the best remembered is the 'Harlem Shake'. In 2013 people began making videos in groups, breaking into berserk fits of dancing when the beat dropped – preceded by the words 'do the Harlem Shake' – on a track by Brooklyn-based producer Baauer. It spread through colleges, workplaces, TV studios, fire stations and even mission control at NASA. Again, it had all the hallmarks of a meme: it was customizable, participatory, and it stopped being funny really, really quickly.

Real-world memes, or 'internet crazes', as confused news anchors tend to call them, have been good, bad and ugly. In 2014, the Ice Bucket

NOW DO THE HARLEM SHAKE

Challenge, in which people filmed themselves tipping a bucket of ice-cold water over their heads, raised $41.8 million for the ALS Association in America, thanks to celebrity endorsements from the likes of Matt Damon, Justin Bieber and then-reality television judge Donald Trump.

In early 2014, however, a more sinister fad known as 'Neknominate' spread through the UK. It was a basic drinking challenge: people were filmed knocking back a pint and then nominating a friend to do the same. Yet as the videos were shared, and the game's notoriety spread, the stakes were raised. People began drinking dangerous amounts and strange concoctions – pints of vodka, engine oil, dead mice, live goldfish and toilet water – and by February five deaths had been blamed on the trend.

You've probably taken part in some real world memes yourself in recent years. Hip-hop dance move the dab – the creation of which is disputed by several artists within the Atlanta music scene – is a phenomenon that first set the world alight in 2015, when American football players started doing it to celebrate scoring. (You know the one: looks like you're diving face first into your elbow to stifle a sneeze.) Since then, everyone's been at it, from politicians to tennis players to every under-16-year-old ever caught in the back of a crowd shot on live TV. Or maybe you've tried bottle-flipping, the practice of tossing a half-filled plastic bottle of water into the air and attempting to land it upright on a table, a craze that became so prolific that schools started banning it. More recently, in 2016, you might have tried the 'Mannequin Challenge', which saw groups of students film themselves frozen completely still, soundtracked by the song 'Black Beatles' by hip-hop duo Rae Sremmurd. Hillary Clinton's presidential

'IN THE MEME-WORLD, AN IDEA DOESN'T JUST CATCH ON, IT SPREADS LIKE A VIRUS'

campaign team filmed a notable example of this during the run-up to the 2016 election, part of their otherwise hugely successful attempt to harness the power of memes to help them win the presidency.

Of course, quirky crazes aren't new to the internet age, but it's impossible to ignore how effectively the worldwide web accelerates them. In the meme-world, an idea doesn't just catch on, it spreads like a virus: articulated in every possible permutation, filling every blank space in our straining, shared brain. In the post-meme age, it's no longer enough to consume media, we have to take part in it, do it our way, reproduce it in a desperate bid to reach a bigger audience.

In fact, even defining a distinction between the 'real world' and the online one is increasingly futile. Our lives exist in both places at the same time, whether you like it or not. In the Age of Lulz, the Anthropomeme, we have turned ourselves into pieces of content. We are all memes.

HEY! LET'S CHAT TO THE HIGH SCHOOL TEACHER WHO TURNS HIMSELF INTO MEMES!

Dave Red, better known to his students as Mr Red, is a physics teacher in Florida. In April 2017, killing time while marking test papers one night, he stumbled across a meme on Facebook. Inspired, he decided to piece together a recreation using a photo of himself instead of the original, an experiment that started him on a wild creative journey. Since then, Dave has recreated roughly thirty memes for the entertainment of his co-workers and the education of his students.

He's dressed up as Gatsby, Salt Bae, Ron Burgundy, the Most Interesting Man in the World, and even donned full clown garb to reproduce the chilling Pennywise from *IT*. Why? Well, you'd have to ask him. What, you want us to do that as well? Typical. How many pages in are we now, and you've done sweet Fanny Adams! Not a single interview! You haven't even captioned a picture! Fine, if you want something doing, do it yourself ...

HI DAVE. WHO ARE YOU?

I teach physics at St Johns River State College, located in St Augustine, Florida. This is my third year at this school. Previously I held the same job at Lander University in Greenwood, South Carolina, for thirteen years.

HOW LONG HAVE YOU BEEN AWARE OF MEMES?

I joined Facebook about six years ago and it seems like memes were either already there, or they were present pretty shortly thereafter. I have no other social media and don't really visit sites like Tumblr and Reddit too often, so my exposure to memes is almost entirely through Facebook.

WHERE DID THE IDEA COME ABOUT TO RECREATE SOME MEMES FOR YOUR STUDENTS?

The first meme re-creation wasn't really for students, it was just for me to express how much I didn't want to grade the stack of exams and labs on my desk at the end of the semester. While procrastinating, I saw a meme that used Gollum expressing a similar feeling with regards to having to do the laundry ('We must do the laundry ... but we hates it!', expressed with pictures of the character first smiling, then angry and hissing). I snapped a couple of photos in my office and made a similar meme.

My basic teaching philosophy is that if they can't learn the material, then no strategy of mine can alter that. If they can learn it (which is overwhelmingly the case), then they WILL learn it so long as I present it clearly and keep their brains awake

TIMETABLE.DOC

MONDAY

AS THEY LEAVE THE EXAM, CHEERS TO ALL MY HATERS

THE GRADE IS YET TO BE POSTED

STRESS

IMPENDING DOOM

TUESDAY

ASSIGNMENT DUE

#

#

I HAVE EXAM ANSWERS

DOWN HERE

ASSIGNING THE FINAL GRADE TO THAT ONE ANNOYING STUDENT

WEDNESDAY

PHYSICS TEST

THURSDAY

RELAX

ENJOY MEMES

OH YOUR LIFE IS RUINED WITHOUT AN A IN THIS CLASS?

TELL ME AGAIN, I'VE NEVER HEARD THAT BEFORE.

and focused on that presentation. The 'keeping them awake' game is one I've been playing for years, well before memes. Sometimes I hand out strange prizes for correct answers, like taco seasoning or soup or pyjama pants. Other times I tell them a bizarre, three-minute story and then we analyse some physical aspect of it. There was a class during which I wore pink every Wednesday for a year as part of a *Mean Girls* theme that ran through the class. The memes are the most recent way of trying to break through the fog that creeps into the mind of students seated in a physics lecture.

WHICH MEME GOT THE BEST REACTION?

From the students at the time, probably Pennywise, the clown from *IT*. That class was probably the best one I've ever had, but they were also very capable of getting themselves stressed out, especially over the final exam. I made that meme and then showed it to them right beforehand, which helped break the tension. Then I handed them the exam, which was titled '*IT* is Finally here' and themed on the clown and movie – though you didn't have to see the movie to answer the questions. The hope was to relax them a little before taking the test since so many of my students really do feel a lot of pressure.

WHICH WAS THE HARDEST TO RECREATE?

I just asked my wife for her opinion on this because, while I had an answer in mind, she is really the one that turns these ideas into reality. She is extremely good at crafts, and making things in general. I will have an idea and tell her and then we will see what we have in the house to make it happen, or maybe make a trip to a thrift or craft store. She has done make-up for these, cut and dyed cheap wigs, helped put together costumes, and then poses me and directs me while taking the photos. This has been, in part, just something for us to do for fun. She agrees with me that the Thanos meme, which we did after they went viral, was the hardest.

WHICH IS YOUR PERSONAL FAVOURITE?

That is a tough one. I really like the Dave Chappelle and Austin Powers memes because they are both simple and, for teachers, very relatable. I like Pennywise because we had to go into work on a weekend to take the picture and the janitor that happened by the room just stopped, turned around and walked out without a word like a scene from *The Office*.

DID YOU EXPECT THEM TO SPREAD ACROSS THE INTERNET IN THE WAY THEY HAVE?

No, I did not expect them to go viral.

- DON'T ASK FOR
  EXTRA CREDIT

ASK FOR EXTRA CREDIT

ONE MORE TIME,
I DARE YOU

$X = XO + VOT$
$+ 1/2AT^2$ I
$(VO)^2 = (VO)^2 +$
$2AX$ $FC = MAC$
$= MV2/R$ $W = FD$
$COS Q = MC$

BETCH

DAVEY IS A FREE ELF!

NEXT WEEK:

THE MEMEING OF
LIFE EQUATION

I had been making them here and there, when an idea struck, for about a year, and like almost everything on my Facebook page, they were set to private. Friends asked me to make them public and once I did, they really took off.

HAVE OTHER TEACHERS CONTACTED YOU?

Many other teachers have been in touch, and they have been very positive when they reach out to contact me. Many of the memes really are aimed at expressing the thoughts and feelings that are common frustrations to teachers.

HOW HAS THIS EXPERIENCE LEFT YOU FEELING ABOUT MEMES?

Overall, I'm glad to have made them and that so many people have enjoyed them. When it comes to memes generally, I have some mixed feelings though. The negative part of that mix comes mainly from the use of memes in relation to political or social issues, because most of those overly simplify complicated issues for the purpose of demonizing someone or some group unfairly. When memes are left to lighter issues, though, I think they can be very expressive. They can provide the body language and facial expression components that are missing with just text. And just like any stand-up comic can tell you, delivery can make the written joke so much better.

AN EXPLORATION INTO THE DARK UNDERBELLY OF THE MEME KINGDOM

R emember earlier, when I said you were a normie. Well, I'm sorry about that.* But I was just trying to prepare you for what was to come. The memes that don't make sense, the jokes that have no end, the unbearable dankness of it all.

What is a dank meme? What makes a meme dank above all others? What is it to be dank?

A dank meme, in simple terms, is a meme that makes fun of memes. At least that's what they were originally. In the years since the term was first used – best guesses date this at some time in 2013 – dank memes have grown from an in-joke into a subculture.

'STEWING IN DISCONTENT'

Before memes, the word 'dank' was conventionally used to describe weed – the nasty, potent sort that makes you feel like your face is trying to finally meet the back of your head after all these years. It's not something you'd likely have heard many seasoned stoners say. 'Dank' is the weed adjective for the wannabe. The bum-fluff-moustachioed dweeb desperately trying to make the right impression in front of his older brother's friends. (Good potential Tinder bio for you, that sentence.)

This inherent lameness might explain why the word became such a good descriptor for memes that set out to make fun of memes. You see, dank memes are a sub-genre that emerged in reaction to the popularity of everyday memes. While people like you were sharing pictures of fist-pumping babies, the sweaty-palmed kids who'd spent hours building meme culture up from nothing were stewing in discontent. Normies were taking memes and sharing them so many times they'd stopped being funny. And even when they stopped being funny, they kept sharing them. Pummelling them, beating them into

STRAP IN NORMIES. >>>>>
HOLD ONTO YOUR BUTTS

SAMPLE TEXT

the ground, mercilessly pounding them until they were dead and then pounding them some more. It was time for a reaction.

Users on Reddit, YouTube and 4Chan began compiling montages of images that looked and sounded like memes, but in practice were a little off. Words were deliberately misspelled, images intentionally distorted, and punchlines were fumbled or missed completely. Quickly, 'dank' became the perfect, ironic way of lowering a set of pixellated black sunglasses and saying 'awesome meme my dude' to the most meaningless content imaginable. Meme-makers on Reddit and 4Chan began making images that used the same basic formats, but stretched the jokes beyond all recognition.

'SAMPLE TEXT'

Gradually, the humour abstracted from parody and became a tone all of its own: twisted, edgy and totally untethered from reality. The dank universe expanded rapidly. Children's characters like Thomas the Tank Engine or Shrek were caught in the crossfire, their surreal visual qualities making them ripe for distortion. Elsewhere a badly animated frog on a unicycle (known as Dat Boi) became an overnight phenomenon, a small gnome from World of Warcraft was turned into an icon, and a loaf of bread from a Christian kids' show was turned into an all-powerful Satanic messenger.

The community that now exists around dank memes goes way beyond a reaction. It's a new subculture entirely, almost eclipsing traditional meme culture in scale and popularity. The 'dank memes' Reddit page has over a million active readers. Dank memes have dragged online humour into a new age of mainstream weirdness, ushering us into an era when a blurred image of Mr Krabs from Spongebob constitutes an understandable reaction to a situation, or politicians debate the influence 'dank memes' are having on the course of an election. In fact, a great deal of the memes you've read about in this book, from trebuchet memes to Harambe, could be described as dank. The armies of dankness, like the Romans before them, have grown into an all-powerful empire – one that shows no sign of falling any time soon.

HOW TO MAKE DANK MEMES

STEP 1. FIND A GREAT PICTURE.

If you're going to make a dank meme, you're going to want to find yourself a pretty funny picture. Like the one we've got here. Then what you're going to want to do is expand it, make it bigger. The bigger you make the picture, the larger the image quality is. That's very important. Pictures are made up of lots of dots, and the bigger the dots, the better the dank meme. Alright, looking good.

STEP 2. THINK OF A HILARIOUS JOKE.

Now what you're going to want to do is think of a funny caption. It's very important this is utterly hilarious: you want people to lose their minds when they see your meme. Memes work best when they are relatable. Spilling coffee or losing your keys: stuff like that. You could try something topical, but remember: think funny. Nobody likes a politics nerd!

STEP 3. CURSE WORDS?

Yes, you can curse in dank memes. These are NOT for kids! Shit on it dude!

STEP 4. PUT THE TEXT SOMEWHERE UNUSUAL.

Okay buster, this might be your first rodeo but we're not making any old meme. This is a dank meme, and as such it's very important you put the text somewhere other than the top or the bottom of the image. Why not try the side? Or a bit below the top. That's more like it.

STEP 5. COLOUR.

Make sure your memes are in colour. Black and white memes WILL fail.

STEP 6. TEST DRIVE.

The only way of getting a good feel for whether or not your dank meme is going to land is to try it out on some friends. What most meme-makers do is print out a few trial versions. That way they can hand examples out to friends and gauge how funny people find them. If you don't have a printer, try hand-drawing some memes.

STEP 7. GET IT ONLINE!

Okay, now it's time to share your dank meme with the internet. There's no right or wrong way of going about this. The best memes grow organically, so don't be afraid of starting small. To kick things off, why not attach it to an email and send it around your colleagues? If that doesn't work, you could upload the meme to a gardening forum or see if your local newspaper will run it on their website. If not, yep, time to build a website from scratch for your meme.

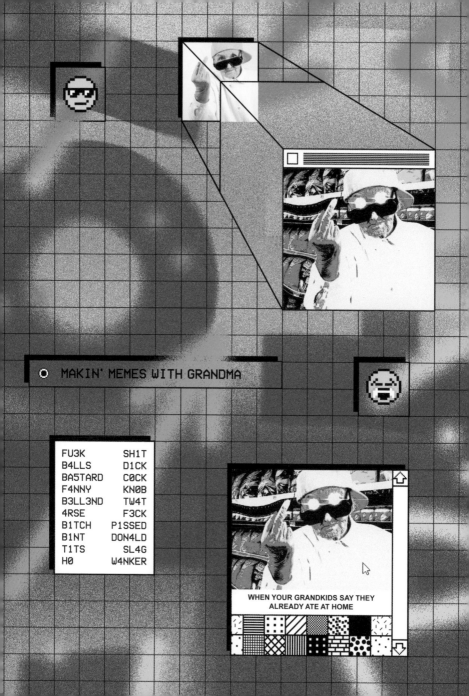

MAKIN' MEMES WITH GRANDMA

FU3K   SH1T
B4LLS   D1CK
BA5TARD   C0CK
F4NNY   KN0B
B3LL3ND   TW4T
4RSE   F3CK
B1TCH   P1SSED
B1NT   DON4LD
T1TS   SL4G
H0   W4NKER

WHEN YOUR GRANDKIDS SAY THEY
ALREADY ATE AT HOME

LIVE

BREAKING NEWS

DESPACITO 9 RELEASED
BY WLADIMIR MELONCHEK

4:20   LEAKED FROM SOVIET UNDERGROUND BUNKER

DEFINING DANKNESS

Things that are 'dank' tend to lack a proper meaning, and in most cases are just silly. A 'dank meme' is a meme that is so stupid and abstract that that is what makes it funny. – CheesyMacaroni85

The word 'dank', in my eyes, means that an idea or image has been indoctrinated into a collective inside joke, this joke now being laughed at by edgelords aka sad and lonely people. – mynemejeffmynenejeff

Well, memes are just the comedic outlet that is used in this day and age. They replaced the old comic strips like Garfield, Peanuts, etc. Using one panel and text to convey the joke. Dank memes are the same only using a darker undertone of comedy. You can think of them as making light-hearted jokes from what can be considered dark material. Comedy is sometimes the best relief for a serious situation. – ZuccFaceberg

My take on this would be that nobody knows. Yes, people might crank out some fancy words and try to explain what dank is, but the truth is, the definition will always be foggy. Rather, it's a term that works as a superiority sign of a particular meme community. – Gaxee

Dank, in my opinion, is synonymous with Excellence. Sure any old mouthbreather can put together a so-called 'meme'. But only a dank-memer can put it together in such a way that not only can the subtleties of the meme be understood by nearly everyone, but also that the meme provides the viewer with a unique perspective on humour. – mkfleet

*I'M NOT

INTRODUCING THE NEW SCHOOL OF WHOLESOME MEMES

ome, my child. Step into the sun and rub the dank-gunk from your eyes. You are safe now, home again.

Meme movements work in reaction to one another. First there were normie memes, the sheer basicness of which begot dank memes. Since then, the impenetrable nature of those has itself birthed a shining new era. Wholesome memes are, as you'd probably guess, memes concerned with spreading good vibes and positive energy. Memes that make you feel warm inside, like a hug, a cup of tea, or pissing your pants.

> '**WHOLESOME MEMES ARE, AS YOU'D PROBABLY GUESS, MEMES CONCERNED WITH SPREADING GOOD VIBES AND POSITIVE ENERGY.**'

They're not totally one-dimensional: these memes started as a joke, taking established, typically negative meme formats – popularized by self-pitying Reddit pages like r/MeIRL – and clumsily applying corny sentiments to them. Memes about failing in life were reappropriated with words of encouragement, and waves of image macros about loving relationships began to emerge in growing numbers.

There were a number of Twitter, Facebook and Instagram pages that sought to collate this new genre of positive vibes. The most successful in numerical terms was r/WholesomeMemes, a Reddit page established in September 2016 by a nineteen-year-old college student from Lewisberg, Pennsylvania. He started the page alongside his then roommate, and it has since become the most popular hub for love and appreciation memes on the internet, with almost two million subscribers at the time of writing.

ONE PUPPER FOR
YOU MY FRIEND

FIG. 15   *HOW ARE YOU FEELING?*

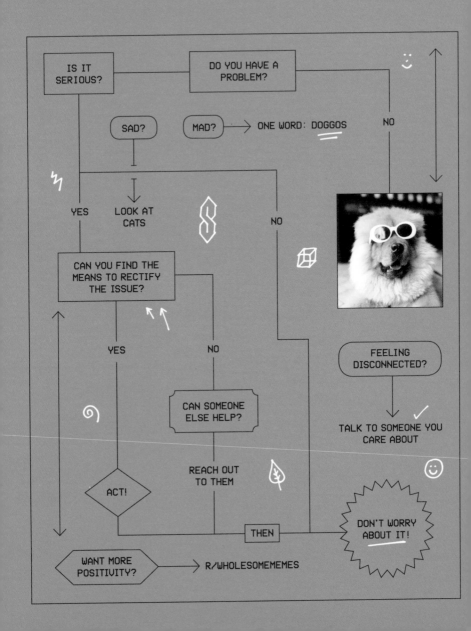

HERE'S THE BIT WHERE WE INTERVIEW SOMEONE!

We spoke to Poppwall – real name Duncan Jones – about the beginnings of r/WholesomeMemes, and what their advent means for the future of the internet. *Run the tape ...*

WHERE DID THIS BEGIN? HAVE YOU ALWAYS BEEN HOOKED ON MEMES?

Honestly, not really. I had a neighbour who would always send me shit. He was one of the edgy kids who was on 4Chan in high school. I was playing sports, never really online. I'm still not really. I only use Reddit to read about the NBA.

SO HOW DOES SOMEONE WHO DOESN'T CARE ABOUT MEMES END UP STARTING A REDDIT PAGE WITH OVER A MILLION SUBSCRIBERS?

I moved in with my friend Carson, and he was always on Reddit. He would always read stuff like *Me IRL*. Some of it started as a reaction to that. Neither of us vibed with the super mopey, self-pity thing going on.

SO WERE THE FIRST WHOLESOME MEMES PARODIES?

People ask this all the time: is it a parody or are you actually that wholesome in real life? I guess it started as a running joke – making negative memes into something more positive. We were producing the worst possible Photoshops we could, just crossing stuff off with really sloppy red lines. If there was a meme that said 'I wanna die', we'd cross that off with red paint and change it to 'Eat ice cream cake'.

Then people realized they genuinely wanted Hallmark memes: memes you can send to your mom, memes you can send to your significant other. It turned into something more serious from there.

HOW YA DOIN' BUD?

WAS ANYBODY ELSE OUT THERE MAKING POSITIVE MEMES BACK THEN?

The idea was floating around. I'd seen a Twitter page called Wholesome Memes – it had maybe four or five memes on it, and nobody had tweeted anything in like a year. We took the ones from Twitter as a base and took it in our own direction. That page started tweeting the ones we were making on Reddit, which was cool.

AND NOW YOU HAVE OVER A MILLION SUBSCRIBERS.

It ballooned into something massive. I hear people talk about it in real life a lot of the time, or I'll see people browsing it in class. It's this huge and surreal thing it's hard to gauge the size of all of a sudden. I have a team of people who help. I can barely keep up with the moderation now.

HOW MUCH MODERATING DOES THE PAGE NEED?

People nitpick very hard. There are a lot of people who make comics and submit them on there. (They were the first people to make art specifically for the page.) I was debating with people I'd never met, who had kindly agreed to help moderate, whether or not comics were memes. People would message like, 'Your definition of memes clearly states that this post here, which has forty upvotes, doesn't count.' I think people really want the page to be a bastion of total purity, but it's hard to be the placid sandy beach people want.

YOU'VE GOT MY UNDYING LOVE AND SUPPORT!

WHY DO YOU THINK PEOPLE GO TO R/ WHOLESOMEMEMES? IS IT TO TAKE THE PISS OUT OF NIHILISTIC MEMES OR ARE THEY GENUINELY USING IT AS A SOURCE OF EMOTIONAL SUPPORT?

I think it really varies. There's a portion of the community that comes in for a takedown of the classic nihilistic meme. I think that was the user base to begin with, and those are most of the angry

messages I get – people telling me we strayed away from that. Then there

are the straight up starry-eyed positive memes. I think you get the most innocent, positive ones rising to the top because they appeal to the most people. If you browse by new, which I do when I'm moderating, you see a lot of people still making really good satirical ones, but they don't go off as much as the classic ones. The median is pretty straight up positive, which is a pretty massive shift in the sort of humour or meaning being communicated in memes.

Memes have moved on from being a weird, edgy thing in the recesses of the internet. I think what this page has shown me is that there are so many people on the internet who might be estranged by more esoteric humour. [Wholesome Memes] works for people who live a normal life, and don't use memes as a form of coded communication. They're not super entrenched in internet subcultures. You don't have to be a certain type of male in your early twenties to understand them.

HAVE YOU EVER BEEN INFILTRATED BY TROLLS?

A GLORY HOLE BUT FOR HOLDING HANDS

FIG. 16 *LOVE POTION* – HOLLY ST CLAIR

We've been raided before. I can't give enough credit to the moderators: some of them have like 900 pages to moderate. They know everything before it's coming. They'll know that people are going to raid and start uploading something foul. We're an easy target.

ANXIETY < YOU

HAVE YOU NOTICED RECURRING THEMES IN WHAT PEOPLE MAKE WHOLESOME MEMES ABOUT?

It's always been about love for whoever, love for whatever. Your parents, your partner, your dog, your kids. It's always cool when people talk about their kids on there. You're like: 'Oh, we've got a user base in their forties and fifties too!' It's funny because almost every piece of human art in history has been about love. We're just a place for people who don't write poems or sonnets, or paint, but express themselves through memes.

HOW DO YOU EXPLAIN THE SUCCESS OF YOUR MEMES?

The memes you see everywhere else on the internet, you'd need a giant blackboard to explain some of them to someone who's never seen it. A lot of the ones on our page, you could print out and hand to your sixty-year-old neighbour and they'd get it immediately. It's the simplicity that makes them so approachable.

WHAT HAS THIS JOURNEY TAUGHT YOU ABOUT THE WAYS PEOPLE USE THE INTERNET?

It's kind of taught me that there's a social hierarchy. Even on the internet there are these norms you have to follow. People say it's faceless, that you could be a dog on the internet – it's not, it's like high school. People act a certain way. They try to be cool. I feel like with memes everyone was trying to be introspective, and bring out some sad depressive side to themselves because they wanted to fit in with the 'in' group on the internet. As soon as we started popping off, I definitely felt people coming round to a way of behaving that was 'cool' but suited them more.

THAT FEELING WHEN YOU FINISH A BOOK

And so we've reached the end. Well done, you've read a whole book! How does it feel? First time for everything, eh? Hopefully now you're less of a fuckin' normie, and feel equipped with the tools and understanding required to navigate the meme kingdom with comfort and ease.

And just maybe, if you've been reading closely, you will understand what this has all been for. The Memeing of Life itself: all of us repeating daily cycles, themselves slight edits on the days before, the weeks and months merely tweaked versions of the generations that came before us.

There is no memeing of life, for life is the biggest meme of all.

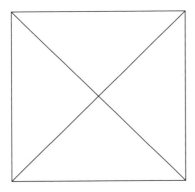

404 PAGE NOT FOUND